LIVES OF FAME & SHAME

FASCINATING FIGURES IN BIBLE HISTORY

ENOCH • LOT • RACHEL • ELIJAH

SAUL • DAVID AND JONATHAN • ASA

HEROD • BARNABAS • TIMOTHY

LIVES OF FAME & SHAME

FASCINATING FIGURES IN BIBLE HISTORY

HERBERT LOCKYER

WHITAKER HOUSE

Unless otherwise indicated, all Scripture quotations are taken from the King James Version of the Holy Bible. Scripture quotation marked (ESV) is taken from *The Holy Bible, English Standard Version,* © 2000, 2001, 1995 by Crossway Bibles, a division of Good News Publishers. Used by permission. All rights reserved. Scripture quotation marked (MOFFATT) is taken from *The Bible: James Moffatt Translation,* © 1922, 1924, 1925, 1926, 1935 by HarperCollins San Francisco; © 1950, 1952, 1953, 1954 by James A. R. Moffatt. Scripture quotation marked (PHILLIPS) is taken from *The New Testament in Modern English,* © 1958, 1959, 1960, 1972 by J. B. Phillips, and © 1947, 1952, 1955, 1957, by The Macmillan Company. Scripture quotations marked (RV) are taken from the Revised Version of the Holy Bible.

Lives of Fame and Shame:
Fascinating Figures in Bible History

ISBN: 978-1-62911-183-4
eBook ISBN: 978-1-62911-184-1
Printed in the United States of America

Whitaker House
1030 Hunt Valley Circle
New Kensington, PA 15068
www.whitakerhouse.com

Library of Congress Cataloging-in-Publication Data

Lockyer, Herbert.
Lives of fame and shame : fascinating figures in Bible history / by Herbert Lockyer.
pages cm
Includes bibliographical references.
ISBN 978-1-62911-183-4 (alk. paper) — ISBN 978-1-62911-184-1 (eBook) 1. Bible — Biography. I. Title.
BS571.L595 2014
220.9'2—dc23
2014031053

1 2 3 4 5 6 7 8 9 10 20 19 18 17 16 15 14

DEDICATION

To the saints in pastorates I held in
Dundee, Hawick, and Bradford,
whose pictures still hang on the walls of my memory.

"History is the essence of innumerable biographies."

—*Thomas Carlyle*

CONTENTS

PREFACE

The Fascination of Biographical Study

One of the most popular and practical, instructive and inspiring, methods of presenting Bible truth is to look at a character and study all that is recorded of him. It is likewise one of the easiest forms of Bible meditation. Thomas Carlyle, in Essays, reminds us, "There is properly no history, only biography," and "Biography is the only true history: history is the garb of biography."

A German proverb has it, "He that would rightly understand a man must read his whole story." Samuel Johnson goes further and says, "Nobody can write the life of a man, but those who have eat and drunk and lived in social intercourse with him." Although such intimate association with Bible characters is impossible, seeing as they died centuries ago, yet we can read their whole story and live with them as they come before us in Holy Writ, until we come to know them very well. If "a well-written life is almost as rare as a well-spent one,"[1] then we are

1. Thomas Carlyle.

fortunate in having many well-written lives in the imperishable record of Scripture.

Some Bible characters, like Enoch, are given a few verses; others, like Ananias, are confined within the limits of a chapter; others, like Adam, stretch over the whole Bible. There are characters, like Luke, who are hidden under their own work; while a figure like Paul asserts himself on our notice in history and biography. There are those, like Absalom, who warn us by their vices; but others, such as David, who inspire us by their virtues. All kinds of characters engage our attention in God's picture gallery—heroes, like Samson; villains, such as Joab; and failures, such as Judas. The most outstanding character in the Bible, apart from the Lord Jesus Christ, is Moses, who had a personal conversation with Jesus in the days of His flesh.

With the aid of a Bible concordance to gather together all the references to a given person, we discover, as Augustine stated it, that "the sacred record, like a faithful mirror, has no flattery in its portraits." How encouraging this is! Here are men and women of like passions as ourselves, and they appeal to the imagination of the average person today because of a similarity of experience. Like these ancient characters, we triumph by faith, as some of them did; or we fail through disobedience and unbelief, as others did. Thus, while all biography is fruitful, Scripture biography is singularly so. The lives of men and women of old may be a continual inspiration or warning to us in these modern times. Allowing for differences of time and place, their temptations and potentials are ours. Their God is our God. But we have a spiritual armory and resources of which they knew little, and thus their defeats should not be ours.

Biography also enables a preacher to deal with doctrinal themes in an interesting way. For instance, dwelling upon

Joseph's life, one can emphasize the overruling providence of God. If the study is David, then he can be used as a living object lesson of divine forgiveness of sin.

The popular former professor of homiletics at Princeton Seminary Dr. Andrew Waterson Blackwood tells in his most valuable treatise *Preaching from the Bible* of an incident in a church he knew of where the pastor had died, and the members came together to pray for a younger man to take the place of the aged leader. During the vacancy, a visiting preacher spoke about Apollos, the eloquent preacher in the early church; and a layman was so impressed with the sermon that he had it printed for free distribution. This led the church to pray for a minister who would preach after the pattern of the one presented. Soon a young preacher was found who answered to the main points of that sermon on Apollos:

- He is eloquent but accurate.
- He is cultured but ardent.
- He is dogmatic but docile.
- He is evangelistic but educational.

If a character is studied for his outstanding feature as a type, Stephen could be profitably used. He was the church's first martyr, and as *martyr* means "witness," the material could be gathered around these points:

- The witness of his life (See Acts 6:3, 5.)
- The witness of his labors (See Acts 6:8.)
- The witness of his lips (See Acts 6:10; 7:2–53.)
- The witness of his looks (See Acts 6:15; 7:55.)
- The witness of his love (See Acts 7:60.)

Biographies, not only of Bible saints, but of saints—and sinners—all down the ages, are often surpassingly instructive. Facts relating to an individual life can often be more readily stated than those of general history. Early preachers made much use of biographical illustration in their sermons. In the bibliography of my own volume *All the Men of the Bible*, students will find a list of authors who have given us some very profitable help along the line of biographical preaching.[2]

The following characters, dealt with somewhat fully, were among several biographical sermons and lectures I gave years ago while in the regular ministry. It is to be hoped they will serve as guides to those who have a desire to pursue such a method of approach.

In warning the church at Corinth not to court disaster through murmuring against God's providence, Paul wrote about the twenty-three thousand Israelites who were destroyed because of their fornication, saying, "*These things happened unto them for ensamples: and they are written for our admonition, upon whom the ends of the world are come*" (1 Corinthians 10:11). We can apply this statement to the biographies of both Bible and church warriors, and say that they were written for our admonition. Emulating their faithfulness, we must, by God's grace, avoid their failures.

In "A Psalm of Life," Longfellow advises that the

Lives of great men all remind us
We can make our lives sublime,

2. Further illustrations of this appealing form of presenting Bible truth can be found in other works of mine, namely *All the Women of the Bible*, *All the Kings and Queens of the Bible*, *All the Apostles of the Bible*, and *All the Children of the Bible*.

And, departing, leave behind us
Footprints on the sands of time;

Footprints, that perhaps another,
Sailing o'er life's solemn main,
A forlorn and shipwrecked brother,
Seeing, shall take heart again.

INTRODUCTION

BIBLE BIOGRAPHIES

What a marvelous portrait gallery God has given us in the holy Word He inspired! The strength and the fascination of such a gallery "lies not in the number but in the variety of its representations, and its highest artistic claim must ever be, that on the canvas of human life it has succeeded in delineating the manifold wisdom of God."[3] No national gallery, however famous, is comparable to God's ancient gallery, with its true portraits of the renowned and the renegade, the conspicuous and the common alike, for all mankind to study. Here we see people who differ in character: some are grave, others gay; some are magnificent, others mean; some are worthy, others wicked. The stories of all should be meditated upon, for in them we can find our own history, in fact and in parable.

Young couples who delight in each other's company and are anticipating marriage should read the love stories of Ruth, Rachel, and Rebekah.

3. George Matheson, *The Representative Men of the Bible.*

All who face severe reverses or bankruptcy should read Job, who lost all, and learn from him the blessing of adversity. "*The* Lord *gave, and the* Lord *hath taken away; blessed be the name of the* Lord" (Job 1:21).

Girls who have a desire to dedicate their precious lives to the Lord will find much to stimulate them in stories of the captive maid, the rise of Esther from obscurity to fame, Lydia, and so forth.

Boys haughty and indifferent, demanding independence and freedom from home ties, can learn an illuminating lesson from the Prodigal Son, who paid dearly for his decision to live as he pleased.

The affluent, who have plenty of this world's goods, can find warning beacon lights in the histories of the rich farmer, the rich young ruler, and the rich man in hell.

The poor and straitened in circumstances will find a companion in Lazarus, who, although he lived on crumbs, went to paradise. Consolation will also be theirs as they think of Jesus, who had nowhere to lay His head.

Here are ten portraits from the divine gallery to look at from every angle in order to discover wherein we resemble them.

CHAPTER ONE

Enoch: The Companion of God Who Never Died

Enoch has one of the shortest yet sweetest biographies in the Bible. There are only two men in heaven who never died—Enoch and Elijah. George Matheson speaks of him as Enoch the Immortal. Reading Genesis 5 is like taking a walk in a cemetery and reading the names inscribed on the tombstones. But this graveyard-like narrative has this peculiarity: The facts of each person are related in the same way. "So-and-so lived so long before so-and-so was born, who lived so long afterward and then died." But when we come to Enoch, the somber monotony is broken, for while his record begins the usual way, there is no account of his death, simply because he did not go in the way of all flesh. One day he was missed and could not be found. God took His walking companion home to be with Himself forever, thereby robbing the undertaker of a mournful task.

HIS HISTORY

Because of the uniqueness of Enoch's life, books, articles, and sermons about him abound. The Bible condenses all it has to say about him in eleven verses, or some 150 words (see Genesis 5:18–24; Hebrews 11:5; Jude 14–15), yet here I am writing almost ten times that amount about him in the cradle of the human race. As we bring together the scanty material we have, the following facts are evident.

First, the name he bore proves that his father, Jared, was rightly guided in his selection of a name, for *Enoch* means "teacher, disciplined, dedicated"—a name fittingly corresponding to his life and witness. Enoch's character reveals that he was a dedicated man whose life was disciplined and whose habits were regulated by the guiding hand of God. His unbroken walk with God made him the effective prophetic teacher Jude declared he was.

Second, Enoch was born and lived in a time of social and communal moral declension, proving that God never leaves Himself without a witness, even in the darkest days of national history. Perhaps somewhere in the world today, a child destined to accomplish great and mighty things for God has been born. In these modern times of ever-increasing degeneracy and apostasy, may God raise up many Enochs to declare, as the patriarch did, divine wrath and judgment upon sinners if they fail to turn from their sin.

Enoch's father's name, *Jared,* means "descending," a word associated with Jordan's springs, implying "rapid descender." Thus, his name was descriptive of the times, which were characterized by the gradual spiritual deterioration of the human race, culminating in the tragic flood. In such a putrid age, Enoch was an arrestive force, for in the midst of increasing corruption and violence, he functioned as the salt of the earth and was doubtless hated because he despised the paint and varnish used to cover up the sin of his age.

Third, Enoch's record is the shortest in the narrative, as was his life; whereas his son, Methuselah, lived the longest—604 years longer than his godly, illustrious father. Enoch lived 365 years—a year for every day of our normal year. The only thing his son was renowned for was his old age. He lived to be 969 years old—hence the proverbial saying "as old as Methuselah." These two characters together teach us that one's life is not to be judged by its length but by its quality. Often, the shortest life is the most fruitful and influential. Jesus was only thirty-three years old when He died. The question is, Is our life telling for God upon the world around? Because "we live in deeds, not years; in thoughts, not breaths,"[4] how important it is to live at the utmost for the Highest?

> He liveth long who liveth well;
> All else is being flung away;
> He liveth longest who can tell
> Of true things truly done each day.[5]

Fourth, another startling innovation, Enoch did not die as did the others who are mentioned in this birth-and-death chapter, with its solemn monotony of a graveyard. When we reach Enoch, there is a startling and blessed break, described for us in a threefold way: *"He was not; for God took him"* (Genesis 5:24). The first phrase suggests how the world regarded Enoch's mysterious disappearance, while the second reveals the divine account of his removal from his home circle. Because Enoch belonged to

---

4. Philip James Bailey, "We Live in Deeds, Not Years."
5. Horatius Bonar, "He Liveth Long Who Liveth Well," 1861.

God, God had every right to take him to be with Himself. (See John 17:24.)

"Enoch...was not found" (Hebrews 11:5). Do not these words conjure up a massive search for a man of such godly character? If no one saw him vanish, family and friends missed him and sought for him without avail. *"He passed away, and, lo, he was not: yea, I sought him, but he could not be found"* (Psalm 37:36). Saints like Enoch are always missed. Are we living so that when we have died, we, too, shall be missed? Robert Murray McCheyne's motto was, "Live so as to be missed when dead." The alarm of the sudden removal of Enoch can illustrate the consternation over the removal of believers at the return of Christ in the air.

"By faith Enoch was translated that he should not see death; and was not found, because God had translated him" (Hebrews 11:5). This further account of Enoch's mysterious disappearance suggests precious truths. First of all, the word "translate" here means to remove from one place or position to another. Paul uses the term in Galatians 1:6 to indicate the sudden change in the religious attitude of the Galatians: *"I marvel that ye are so soon removed from him that called you into the grace of Christ unto another gospel."* When Enoch was translated, he found himself immediately transferred from earth to heaven. In his miraculous and supernatural ascension, he was removed from the position of an earth dweller to that of a companion with God in His high and holy temple.

Perhaps this is what might have happened if Adam had not sinned and his descendants had remained sinless—perhaps they would have been suddenly translated from an earthly existence to a heavenly one at God's command. As we shall later see, Elijah shared the unique experience of Enoch of going directly to heaven in his body. If Christ should return today, countless thousands of regenerated men and women would likewise go to heaven without dying.

Oh, joy! oh, delight! should we go without dying.[6]

The purpose or result of Enoch's translation was that he should not see or undergo death before the judgment of the flood. As such, he was a type of the true church translated before the great tribulation overtakes a godless, guilty world. For some three hundred years, he had habitually walked with God; therefore, heaven was in his heart, and his body had no need to rest in foreign soil before its resurrection. Because Jesus was perfect in creation, in character, and in probation, He could have gone straight to heaven from the Mount of Transfiguration. But, for the joy of having myriads of redeemed hearts sharing His glory, He turned from the mount and endured the cross.

One devotional writer has suggested that, as very close friends, God and Enoch were in the habit of walking together each day, and that one day, God said, "Enoch, you have walked a long way with Me today; why not come home with Me?" Thus, God took him to His abode, thereby extending an earthly walk into eternal companionship.

The historian tells us that *"before his translation,"* Enoch had the indisputable testimony *"that he pleased God"* (Hebrews 11:5). Walking with Him and getting to know His will, Enoch's delight was to do God's will. Oh, that it might be said of each of us, "He pleased God"! Are we well-pleasing to Him? *"Without faith it is impossible to please him"* (Hebrews 11:6). Faith was exhibited by Enoch in his walking with God and in his passion to please Him. Faith alone can create such a close, personal relationship as that which existed between God and Enoch. The phrase *"had this testimony"* (Hebrews 11:5) preserves the force

6. H. L. Turner, "Christ Returneth," 1878.

of the perfect tense *"he hath had witness borne to him"* (RV); and such a testimony still stands on record. At the heart of Christ's gospel is His declaration, *"Whosoever liveth and believeth in me shall never die"* (John 11:26).

HIS CHARACTER

From the passages associated with the career of Enoch, we can glean one or two lessons regarding the divine ideal for our witness here on earth. First of all, it is interesting to observe how and when Enoch was called to work and walk with God. We have no way of knowing whether Enoch was a man of faith *before* the birth of Methuselah, which took place when Enoch was sixty-five years of age. What is clearly evident is that his walking with God commenced after the birth of his son. Before the child was born, he may have believed and worshipped God, as Abel had; but *after* Methuselah's birth, something happened in Enoch's heart, and a closer walk that continued for three centuries commenced. From that time on, he and God became agreed companions as never before. *"Can two walk together, except they be agreed?"* (Amos 3:3).

The inference, then, is that the coming of this child into his life and home marked a spiritual crisis, and it awakened Enoch to a sense of his responsibility to Him who had given him a son. Often, spiritual experiences are associated with various circumstances. With Enoch, it was the birth of a child. With Isaiah, it was the death of a king. *"In the year that king Uzziah died I saw also the Lord"* (Isaiah 6:1). Both the cradle and the grave have been used of God to draw those standing around them nearer to Himself. Crises have resulted in many conversions.

Twice over we are told that Enoch *"walked with God"* (Genesis 5:24) or *"lived close to God"* (MOFFATT). The verb used for *"walked"* means "to go on habitually." Do you not covet such a short and signal biography? There was nothing intermittent about this marvelous friendship between the Creator and one of His creatures. There was no break in this remarkable companionship. Enoch lived a life of continual—full and unbroken—communion with his heavenly Companion. The lost privilege and forfeited position of Eden were regained and held by Enoch, who did not have Adam's perfect environment. In spite of the increasing godlessness of the time in which he lived, this friend of God did not yield to the seductive inducements of his age.

At the end of each day's walk, Enoch found his difficulties surmounted, conquests gained, and new songs of triumph to sing. Although compassed about with iniquitous contemporaries, this companion of God went on from strength to strength. His character was deepened, and his pure soul mounted to experiences still higher and broader and more satisfying and spiritual. There was, of course, a goal to crown the exercise of walking with God for three centuries. At the close of his earthly walk, the Celestial City was reached, and Enoch entered the perfect life his heavenly Companion of the road had treasured up for him.

That memorable walk, then, was gloriously maintained in spite of a corrupt and degenerate civilization. What was possible for this seventh man from Adam in the dawn of human history may be deemed impossible in the cesspool of iniquity surrounding us today. Yet we have provisions to draw upon that Enoch did not have. We live on this side of the cross and in the dispensation of the Holy Spirit, making vast resources available to us to become more than conquerors over the world, the flesh, and the devil.

Enoch's walk with God was maintained in spite of family ties and home cares. Such responsibilities should not interfere with our walk with God. Our home life can be peaceful and fragrant only as each member strives to live in uninterrupted fellowship with Him who *"setteth the solitary in families"* (Psalm 68:6).

Enoch's walk with God was sustained even amid the obligations of his secular employment. In all probability, he was a proprietor of cattle and lands and a master of servants; yet, in spite of the trials and problems that must have arisen, his life was unspotted. Because of the boundless grace and power of God, there is no legitimate sphere in which it is too hard to be a Christian. Saints could be found even in Caesar's household. Too often businessmen fail to put the principles of Christianity into practice. They shrink from the cost of true discipleship.

Enoch's walk with God was not hindered in any way by the growing spiritual deterioration of his times. Jude reminds us that Enoch was a prophet who was not afraid to declare to the ungodly the wrath of God they would experience. Although he lived in a vitiated atmosphere, breathing the purer air of heaven, he rebuked the works of darkness. Thus his record gives the lie to the idea that it is impossible to be a Christian after the New Testament ideal in a complex and Christless world like ours. If anything, the world today is more degenerate than it was in Enoch's time, yet it is easier for us to wear the white flower of a blameless life. Do we not have a fuller knowledge of the will and program of God and a fuller measure of the grace of Christ and power of the Holy Spirit than Enoch had?

As the shadows of Enoch's predicted judgment are gathering around our godless world, there are two perils we can easily glide into if we are not prayerfully watchful:

THE PERIL OF BEING INFLUENCED BY OUR SURROUNDINGS

Beyond doubt, Enoch was counted odd or antiquated by those of his generation because of the saintliness of his life. His striving to please God, we can be assured, displeased men. Having chosen to walk with God, he could not walk with the ungodly. It takes a living fish to swim against the stream; and rather than being caught in the whirlpool of corruption, Enoch lived a life contrary to others. He preferred divine company to worldly companions. It is to be feared that we often find it easier to float with the stream, to accommodate ourselves to our environment, or refuse to separate ourselves from worldly pleasures and pursuits. There are some who, like a chameleon, try to be at home in their surroundings, religious or otherwise. They think it clever to be "good mixers."

THE PERIL OF THINKING IT IS TOO HARD TO LIVE FOR GOD

What God has enabled one to do, He can enable another to do, for His grace and power are for each and all. Like Enoch, we, too, can walk with God by faith; and, like Enoch, we, too, can throw into greater contrast, by our holiness, the evil of the day in which we live. If we follow Enoch's example and walk habitually with God in spite of uncongenial and unresponsive surroundings, then before long, we, too, shall not be found. At the return of the Savior, we will be translated from the dusty lanes of earth to the golden streets above.

Walk in the light: and thou shalt own
Thy darkness passed away,
Because that light hath on thee shone
In which is perfect day.[7]

7. Bernard Barton, "Walk in the Light," 1826.

CHAPTER TWO

Lot: The Compromising Mayor of Sodom

The story of Lot is one of the most tragic in the Old Testament. What a blemished biography Scripture gives us of this pioneer of faith who made a wrong choice! From the portrait Peter gives us of Lot, it would seem as if he had never compromised with the wicked ways of Sodom, for the apostle speaks of him as a "*just*" man, a "*righteous man,*" whose "*righteous soul*" (2 Peter 2:7–8) was vexed by the filthy, unlawful deeds of the Sodomites. The Revised Version repeats the word "*righteous*" three times. "[God] *delivered righteous Lot, sore distressed by the lascivious life of the wicked (for that righteous man dwelling among them, in seeing and hearing, vexed his righteous soul from day to day with their lawless deeds).*" Such an evaluation of Lot's character presents him as one who was not such a "bad Lot" after all. But let us see how this so-called righteous man is presented in the opening book of the Bible. (See Genesis 13; 14; 19.)

Both Abraham and Lot, as well as Sodom, are typical of many aspects of our spiritual witness and experiences.

Abraham is conspicuous as the man of faith, separated from the world, separated unto God, and whose eyes looked for the things unseen and eternal.

Lot, unlike his spiritual uncle, was a man of the world and of sense, a selfish, carnal, compromising character, who looked only at things seen and temporal. Therefore, Lot has no place in the catalog of the heroes of faith in Hebrews 11.

Sodom is a fitting type of our sinful, wicked world. Henry David Thoreau, an American writer and philosopher of the eighteenth century, wrote, "Wherever men have lived there is a story to be told," and what a story of sordidness and destruction Sodom tells! All cities and citizens that are Sodom-like in character face a doom similar to that city of old from which Lot was divinely rescued.

Two things are prominent in the portrait given of Lot, namely, the gain of position and the loss of power.

THE GAIN OF POSITION

Lot, as the sacred record tells us, was the son of Abraham's brother Haran, who died before Abraham and Lot left the Ur of the Chaldees. Being childless, Abraham was drawn to his fatherless nephew and possibly looked upon him as an heir to his possessions. Although "there was nothing of the originality and the initiative of Abraham in Lot," the young man did believe in his uncle's God and was one with him in the great venture into the unknown. Under divine inspiration, Peter called him "righteous Lot," which implies that he'd had some knowledge and experience of God. "The righteous man" of the Old Testament would be the equivalent of a "Christian" under grace.

Lot, then, started well. After his father's death, Abraham was left with the inheritance of his father, Terah (see Genesis 11:31), and his nephew Lot followed him into Canaan. (See Genesis 11:32; 12:4–5.) When, in disobedience to the divine call, Abraham went into Egypt, Lot went with him and returned with him to the place where their tent had been at the beginning. (See Genesis 12:10; 13:4.) Lot, then, ran well at the beginning, but he was hindered in the race. (See Galatians 5:7.) He began in the Spirit, but, as we shall see, he ended in the flesh.

The first stage in Lot's downward career came when he made a selfish choice. A man discovers what kind of man he is in choosing how to handle the opportunities and alternatives put before him. There are three marked steps in the journey toward Sodom: Lot chose to go, he pitched his tent toward Sodom, and he sat at the gate. (See Genesis 13:10–11; Psalm 1:1.) Lot shared the prosperity of Abraham, because he willingly followed his uncle when the call came to him to leave the land of their nativity for the land God was to show him. But "*the land was not able to bear them, that they might dwell together: for their substance was so great, so that they could not dwell together*" (Genesis 13:6).

Then there came the strife between their respective herdsmen, leading Abraham to offer Lot his freedom and the choice of the whole land before them. How magnanimous it was of Abraham to give Lot the first pick, which, by right of seniority, should have been his! (See Genesis 13:7–9.) Greedily, Lot chose the well-watered plain before him, where Sodom was situated; and in so doing, he separated himself from his revered relative and friend, whose assistance he was yet to need. Lot should never have severed such a strong link with a God-chosen man like Abraham, thereby removing himself from the sphere of spiritual and moral influence that had nurtured him up to this time. If God has given us the friendship of a godly, strong, and stalwart person, let us see to it that nothing comes between to mar such beneficial companionship.

The gospel of the world is, "Take care of number one"; each man for himself, and the devil take the hindermost. When Abraham gave Lot first choice, the honorable thing for him to do would have been to say, "No, Uncle; because you are my senior, you make the choice. I am here with all this substance because of you. I am reaping part of the blessing God pronounced upon you before we left home." But such nobility was not characteristic of Lot, who appears as a "mean Lot" in his selfish choice, which, ignorantly, he thought was the better choice as he pitched his tent toward Sodom. (See Genesis 13:12.)

The citizens of Sodom were "*wicked and sinners before the* LORD *exceedingly*" (Genesis 13:13). Isaiah speaks of the shamelessness of the men of Sodom. (See Isaiah 3:9.) Jeremiah condemned them for their evil influence and idolatry. (See Jeremiah 23:14.) Ezekiel exposed their pride, satiety, idleness, and neglect of the needy. (See Ezekiel 16:49.) Peter wrote of their filthy conversation, or manner of life. (See 2 Peter 2:7.) Jude singles out their fornication. (See Jude 7.) If only Lot had seen the putridness of this city in that well-watered plain and had taken a different road, what a different story would have been his.

Pitching *near* Sodom, it was not long before Lot was *in* it, when he would experience the disaster of his selfish choice, for he was plundered of his goods and taken prisoner by warring and avaricious kings. Word reached Abraham as to his nephew's tragic condition, and he hastened to deliver him from his predicament. One would have thought that Lot, having been freed by Abraham, who recovered all of his goods, would have come to his senses and, after thanking his aged uncle for rescuing him, would have confessed how he needed him. But no, graciousness and gratitude were not in his makeup, and so the breach between the two was not healed. (See Genesis 14:1–16.)

THE GAIN OF PUBLIC OFFICE

Once settled in sinful Sodom, Lot was not long in becoming a prominent figure in civic affairs. The world is ever ready to engulf and honor the carnal Christian. *"Lot sat in the gate of Sodom"* (Genesis 19:1). "Sitting in the gate" is an Eastern phrase used of a person with an office equivalent to our judge or mayor, a person whose responsibilities were the settling of disputes between inhabitants and the reception of visitors as the representative of the city's hospitality. It was in the latter capacity that Lot welcomed and entertained the two angels sent by God to warn Sodom of its doom. (See Genesis 19:1, 12–13.) Thus the onetime pilgrim became the provost. One wonders whether Lot thought he could change the morals of the city by living in it and taking office in it. If so, he embarked on a futile and dangerous policy. The man who had the most influence upon Sodom was the man outside it (see Genesis 14:16), who, as a good soldier, did not entangle himself with the affairs of this life (see 2 Timothy 2:4) and believed that the friend of this world is an enemy of God (see James 4:4). Abraham was a "separated man."

Oh, the peril of position! Too often when a professed believer gets on in the world, he goes backward in his spiritual life; yet this should not be. Consecrated good men are needed in all public offices; but, because of the corrupted ways of life and of society, it is nearly impossible for a spiritually minded person to retain his spirituality. Satan tried to lure Jesus with the promise of position: *"All these things will I give thee"* (Matthew 4:9). But the proffered possessions were strongly despised by Him who was tempted as we are. Many have found ambition to be ruinous! So much has been sacrificed to be somebody and to have something. Is it not far better to be a nobody here and a somebody there? Too often, a coveted career ends in an early coffin.

THE GAIN OF A WIFE

In Luke 17:32, our Lord refers to Lot's wife, who was not mentioned in Lot's story until he was commanded to take his wife and daughters out of the cesspool of iniquity: "*And when the morning arose, then the angels hastened Lot, saying, Arise, take thy wife, and thy two daughters, which are here; lest thou be consumed in the iniquity of the city*" (Genesis 19:15). Her presence in the home is, of course, inferred in the conversation between Lot and the angels. (See Genesis 19:8, 12, 14.) When Abraham left his country, his wife, Sarah, accompanied him, but nothing is said about Lot's wife. It would seem as if he were a bachelor until he settled in Sodom and that he took a Sodomite to wed, and that she is one of the unnamed women in the Bible. Perhaps it was she who gradually brought Lot over to the life and ways of the Sodom she dearly loved—and in which she eventually died because she was too reluctant to leave.

If Lot did marry a Sodomite woman, then this was a further step in his continually compromising journey. Uniting with such a godless woman was an act of disobedience to the revealed will of God. By yoking himself to an unbeliever, Lot, as a professed believer in God (see Genesis 19:18–19), courted disaster. The kind of daughters Lot's wife bore proves her evil influence as a mother. When two marry, it should be in the Lord. But when a Christian marries a non-Christian, such a union is *not* in (or of) the Lord. Often, the Christian loves the non-Christian and thinks that by marrying the unbelieving partner, he/she can win her/him over for the Lord. While this effort has been known to succeed, in the majority of cases, there develops strife and trouble and constant friction, with one pulling one way, and the other, the opposite.

Compromise in respect to marriage, then, can prove disastrous, as it did in the case of righteous Lot, who should have chosen a righteous wife and lived together with her as one in the Lord.

THE GAIN OF MATERIAL POSSESSIONS

Like Abraham, Lot lived in a tent as they journeyed from Haran into the land of Canaan. (See Genesis 13:5.) But once in Sodom, he no more experienced the confinement and lack of facilities of a rough outdoor life, for Lot now possessed a house. It must have been a large one to hold his family, give shelter to his servants, and entertain strangers. (See Genesis 19:2–3.) Once a sojourner, Lot was now a comfortable settler, living no longer by faith but by sight. Having brought considerable wealth with him in flocks, herds, tents, and herdsmen, his trade with the Sodomites must have added to his riches. But, unlike his uncle, Lot made investments in God that were not very large. Pitching his tent toward Sodom, he soon lost the pilgrim life and, as the city's mayor, added to his possessions.

It is not wrong, of course, to have earthly possessions. The sin comes when such possessions have us and dominate our life. Too often, spiritual impoverishment follows the enlargement of our borders. The warning is, *"If riches increase, set not your heart upon them"* (Psalm 62:10). It is somewhat surprising what airs even professing Christians can cultivate if they rise a few steps on the social ladder because of the acquisition of greater wealth.

A Christian in the world is necessary and God-designed; but the world in a Christian is wrong and disastrous. What truth is wrapped up in the old proverb "More men are killed by meat than poison." How we have to guard against the perils of gain! When gold is substituted for God, and faith is forfeited for fame, and desire for gifts kills love for the Giver, barrenness of soul is bound to follow. Lot's prominent place in the questionable society of Sodom cost him his spirituality. He found that the corruption of a city was the wrong kind of soil in which to cultivate the flower of holiness.

THE LOSS OF POWER

How paltry the material gains of Lot in Sodom appear when balanced against the spiritual losses he sustained! Paul could triumphantly declare, "*What things were gain to me, those I counted loss for Christ*" (Philippians 3:7). It is said of Moses that he esteemed the reproach of Christ greater riches than the treasures of Egypt. (See Hebrews 11:26.) But poor Lot esteemed his position and possessions in Sodom greater riches than the unclouded vision of God's face, and consequently he lost so much of imperishable value.

HE LOST THE POWER OF HIS SPIRITUALITY

Being an important figure in Sodom, Lot had to live like a Sodomite, although inwardly he knew that such a course was not right, for Peter says that his righteous soul was vexed by all he saw and heard. (See 2 Peter 2:7–8.) Yet the fact remains that he surrendered the altar of God at Bethel for the idols of Sodom. What a tragic exchange! When the angels forced him to leave the doomed city, we read that "Lot lingered." (See Genesis 19:16.) What kept him back? Was it that which led him there, namely, material advantages? The deeper into the life of Sodom he plunged, the firmer its grip on him became. How imperative it is for us to learn how to hold loosely to things of earth, having little to bind us to a doomed world!

Some idea of Lot's spiritual loss can be judged by the actions of the angels who came to warn him of Sodom's destruction. They would not accept the offered hospitality of his home but preferred to stay out in the street of the city. The kind of home he had made lacked the atmosphere necessary and congenial for the entertainment of visitors from heaven. "Lot knew too much about Sodom to be happy with it: and he knew too much about God to be fully happy in Sodom, and so he let his life be spoiled."

HE LOST HIS POWER WITH ABRAHAM

Had Lot kept near his uncle, a more commendable story would have been his. How fortunate he was to have had a grandfather like Terah and a relative like Abraham! But now that he was somebody in Sodom, having made a good start with the mighty patriarch, he had no further use for the wise old man whom the Lord blessed in all things. How heartless it was to separate from Abraham and sever himself from the safeguard of such a holy relationship! Now in Sodom, Lot must have had companions corresponding to his ambitions, so he mingled freely with the men of Sodom, just as backsliding Peter sat down among those who were crying out for the blood of Jesus.

Have you noticed how carnal Christians shun the fellowship of true Abrahams? Becoming more at home with those who are worldly minded, they shun the company of those who are separated unto God. When Lot turned himself adrift from Abraham, he deliberately cut himself off from godly influences that would have made him, like his uncle, *"the Friend of God"* (James 2:23). We say that "a man is known by the company he keeps." (See Proverbs 13:20.) How true! Show me the kind of company you like best, and I'll tell you how near to, or far from, Christ you are. Are you glad when spiritually minded friends say to you, "Let us go into the house of the Lord"? The well-known hymn reminds us that if we would "take time to be holy," we must "Make friends of God's children, help those who are weak, / Forgetting in nothing His blessing to seek.[8]

HE LOST HIS POWER WITH THE SODOMITES

In coming down to the level of the Sodomites' unlawful deeds, Lot surrendered what influence he had had over them. When he tried to prevent the corrupt men of Sodom from committing sodomy with the two angels—sodomy being the legalized homosexuality of today, or, to put it as Paul did in no uncertain terms, *"The men, leaving the natural use of the woman, burned in their lust one toward another; men with men working that which is unseemly, and receiving in themselves that recompense of their error which was meet"* (Romans 1:27)—they rebuked Lot, saying, *"Stand back....This one fellow came in to sojourn, and he will needs be a judge: now will we deal worse with thee, than with them"* (Genesis 19:9).

What an unbecoming way that was to treat their magistrate who had sat in the gate! But those men knew that Lot, in spite of his professed faith in the Lord, was a compromiser, trying to make the best of both worlds; therefore, his appeal to them not to commit a foul deed carried no weight. So destitute was Lot of spiritual influence that he was not able to take one convert to God out of the city. All the Sodomites, with the exception of his two daughters, perished in the doom overtaking the city. Had it not been for Abraham's intercession for the city in

8. William D. Longstaff, "Take Time to Be Holy," 1882.

which it was impossible to find ten righteous men (see Genesis 18:32), Lot himself might also have perished in the destruction of Sodom. The further removed we are from the ways of the world, the greater our spiritual influence is over those who are of the world. As Mary Slessor once put it, "Complete separation from the world spells power from God."

HE LOST HIS POWER WITH HIS WIFE

Lot suffered much because of his compromise in entering into an unholy union with a woman of Sodom. The kind of wife and mother she was can be seen in the gross immorality of the two daughters she had brought up. As for Lot, we can see how far he had fallen from grace, when he was willing to hand over his two virgin girls to the men of the city to rape, in order to protect his visitors. When, ultimately, the brimstone and fire from the Lord out of heaven fell upon Sodom and Gomorrah, and the angels hastened Lot to flee with his wife and daughters, they said to him, "*Look not behind thee*" (Genesis 19:17). But the wrench was too much for Lot's wife, who, although she was forced to flee Sodom, had Sodom very much in her heart and "*looked back…and she became a pillar of salt*" (Genesis 19:26). Lot had no influence over her in such an hour of crisis.

How different it was with Abraham when it came to the choice of a wife for his beloved son Isaac! Although he was living among idolaters, he did not look for a partner among their eligible young women but made his servant swear that he would "*not take a wife for my son of the daughters of the Canaanites, among whom I dwell: but thou shalt go unto my country, and to my kindred, and take a wife for my son Isaac*" (Genesis 24:3–4 RV). And we know the rest of the story—how the servant was led of God to Abraham's own brother Nahor, whose beautiful virgin granddaughter Rebekah proved to be God's choice for Isaac. (See Genesis 24:10–28.)

When our Lord used the catastrophe overtaking Sodom as a type of the divine judgment that will overtake a guilty, godless world, He said, *"Remember Lot's wife"* (Luke 17:32). This exhortation of His was a warning that to look back may have fatal results. Those who put their hands to the plough and look back are not fit for the kingdom, said the One whose eyes were set steadfastly toward the cross at Calvary. (See Luke 9:62.)

What a tragedy it is when, because of his worldly compromises, a professing Christian husband has no spiritual influence over the one nearest to him, and vice versa. Ruth was so swayed by the religion of her mother-in-law, Naomi, that she said, *"Thy people shall be my people, and thy God my God"* (Ruth 1:16).

HE LOST HIS POWER OVER HIS CHILDREN

Lot's two daughters, born in Sodom, married Sodomites who perished in the flames. If their father's righteous soul was vexed over the ungodliness of the men of Sodom, he had no influence in preventing his daughters from marrying two of the men who must have been very corrupt, seeing that they were not allowed to leave the doomed city with their wives. One can judge the kind of women they were, having such husbands. That they were thoroughly immersed in the evil morals of Sodom is seen in what happened in that cave when they got their father drunk and committed such a dreadful sin (see Genesis 19:33–38), making their own father the father of their children. This terrible episode abruptly ends the dark story of Lot's compromising life.

What a tragedy it is when religious parents lose the power to influence their children for God! Inconsistency, worldly compromise, lack of affection and understanding, or too rigid a discipline often drive children away from the true life God would have His own to live. If Lot was vexed over the way his children grew up in such a mire of iniquity, he could have saved himself the vexation of the righteous soul that Peter said he had by leaving Sodom and its corrupt ways and joining up with godly Abraham again. However, he was too deeply immersed in Sodom's life and ways that he stayed there until destruction fell. "*Come out from among them, and be ye separate*" (2 Corinthians 6:17) is the only way to regain lost spiritual influence, as many carnal-minded Christian parents have proved. When a truly spiritual home is created, what a joy it is to see children growing up in the fear of the Lord and "*like olive plants round about thy table*" (Psalm 128:3). There is beauty all around when godliness pervades our home life.

HE LOST HIS POWER OVER HIS RELATIVES

What a bitter experience it is when one loses the reverence, respect, and love of relatives! This, also, was part of the price Lot paid for his compromising weakness. When he received the angelic warning regarding the overthrow of Sodom, he sought to impress his sons-in-law with the extreme gravity of the situation—but with what effect? "*He seemed as one that mocked unto his sons in law*" (Genesis 19:14). They looked on him as a sorry old man who was unnecessarily scared. The life of their father-in-law contradicted his professed faith in God and hatred for sin; thus, Lot's declaration of the doom of the city fell on deaf ears, the result being that these two young Sodomites perished with the rest.

In his despair, Samson cried unto the Lord; his prayer was heard, and power was restored. (See Judges 16:28–29.) Not so with Lot. He had left God and had lost his life in worldly gain, and his urgent witness was spurned and treated with contempt. The godless never heed or believe the warnings of those who live a compromising life. After parleying with sin and the world, their pleading for sinners to repent is scorned. Let us beware, lest in the gain of position, possessions, and influence, we lose our power to warn others to flee from the wrath to come.

Lot may have added greatly to his riches and prestige in Sodom, but in the end, he left it a pauper, both materially and spiritually. As he escaped for his life, all he possessed was destroyed, save for the two ungodly daughters who had left with him. He had lost his goods and his godliness, as well as his opportunity to turn any of the Sodomites from the evil of their ways. For the spiritual welfare of the city, "righteous Lot" did absolutely nothing. Even when he broached religion, the people would not listen. What a sorrowful story!

HE LOST HIS POWER WITH GOD

Among Lot's spiritual losses through material gains, one was the most tragic of all—the severance of fellowship with God. In all Old Testament references to Lot, there is not a single word from him about God or of any faith he had until any intervention or intercession on his part to save Sodom from its doom was too late. Lot was commanded to escape for his life to *"the mountain"* (Genesis 19:17). Lot then uttered his first recorded reference to the Lord, who had been so merciful to him—and it was in the form of a protest! *"Oh, not so, my Lord"* (Genesis 19:18). Pleading the grace and mercy of the Lord, he tried to trade on His goodness in delivering him from the burning city.

This worldly-wise, unspiritually minded man argued with the Lord about severing him completely from the wicked city. Being exiled to a mountain was too dreadful to contemplate, for some evil might befall him there! So he brazenly argued, *"This city is near to flee unto, and it is a little one: Oh, let me escape thither, (is it not a little one?) and my soul shall live*" (Genesis 19:20). Mercifully, the Lord responded to this request, and Lot fled to Zoar (which means "little one"); and although the sun rose as he entered the small city within easy distance of Sodom, it does not seem as if the Sun of Righteousness had risen in his heart. Still the compromising Lot, he did not want to go too far from the city. There is no record of any return to the altar or to Bethel, where, along with Abraham, he had called upon the name of the Lord. (See Genesis 13:3–4.) If Lot died "a righteous man," he was saved yet so as by fire. (See 1 Corinthians 3:13.)

There is a pathetic touch to the phrase "*Abraham gat up early in the morning to the place where he stood before the Lord: and he looked toward Sodom and Gomorrah*" (Genesis 19:27–28). As he saw the country enveloped as with "*the smoke of a furnace*" (verse 28), the old patriarch must have had painful thoughts about his nephew, who had started out so well on the pilgrim journey but did not choose to finish it.

The sad story of Lot is a beacon light to all who name the name of the Lord, to beware of compromise in any shape or form. They must be on their guard about taking the first step, which, if taken, leads to another and another and on to a disastrous end. In the goodness of God, He sent His angels to deliver Lot out of Sodom, and He alone can take us by the hand and bring us out of the pollution of the world, if we have succumbed to it, and restore our soul. Peter tells us that God is able to deliver us out of temptation. Backsliding, carnal Christians must return to Bethel and renew their covenant with God, if, like Abraham, they would have God as their "*shield, and…exceeding great reward*" (Genesis 15:1).

If, like the angelic messengers, we are sent into Sodom to warn sinners of their doom—that if they linger, they will die in their sins—then God will keep us safe from its filth and iniquity. The sole mission of those angels was to declare the mind of God as to the destruction of the city, and to pluck four out of it before the fire fell. For those of us who are separated from the world, our constant message to it must be, "Escape thou for thy life! Flee to the mountain of Calvary before judgment overtakes such a godless world!"

CHAPTER THREE

Rachel: The Wife Who Wept Because She Was Barren

Any student of homiletics knows that there is a tendency on the part of some preachers to widely and wildly spiritualize Scripture. Origen, one of the church fathers of the third century, is said to have been the originator of Christian allegorizing; and from then on, fanciful treatment of biblical themes became popular. Some of the titles early preachers gave to the sermons were ludicrous, while the sermons themselves were often imaginative flights of oratory. Even today there are those who, most ingeniously, can find types of Christ and emblems of the spiritual life in almost every part of the Bible.

That there is a sane and warrantable spiritualizing of Scripture is clear from Scripture itself. The writer to the Hebrews tells us that the ordinances and offerings associated with the tabernacle of old were illustrations of spiritual truth or *"figures of the true"* (Hebrews 9:24). The same applies to persons such as, for instance, Melchizedek and Christ. In effective preaching and teaching of Scripture, the first principle is *interpretation,* then *application* within reason—a principle our meditation of Rachel is meant to prove.

As a pastor stands at the portal of his winter's work, or an evangelist commences a gospel campaign, he finds it incumbent upon himself to enunciate a few spiritual guidelines for successful soulwinning. What more impressive basis for appeal to devotion to such a God-honoring task can be found than that of Rachel's heartbreaking cry, "*Give me children, or else I die*" (Genesis 30:1)? If there is to be a breath of revival, Christians must have a great passion for souls. All who form a church or unite in revival effort must cry, "Give us spiritual children, implant within our hearts a passion to save the lost, make us soulwinners, or else we die!" When any church travails like this, she brings forth children. Rachel was not the only woman in the Bible to weep because of her barrenness, but we take her story, seeing that it suggests spiritual parallels for those who seek to win the souls around them for the Savior who died, that those lost in sin might be saved.

Rachel herself was the younger daughter of Laban, whose great-uncle was Abraham. Laban's sister was Rebekah, who became the wife of Isaac. While caring for her father's sheep at the well of Haran, she saw a young man approaching and soon discovered it was her cousin Jacob, the son of her aunt Rebekah. Fleeing from his brother Esau's vengeance, he had followed his mother's advice and had come to his uncle as a fugitive. Jacob saluted Rachel with a kiss of frank and fearless affection; they were cousins, and their love was unreserved. There seemed, however, to be a deeper love at first sight, and that meeting at the well was the beginning of a deep and long devotion. In the Bible gallery, theirs is the first recorded courtship, and it grew out of a cousinly relationship. The surest sexual love is that which begins and continues in a mutual friendship.

RACHEL WAS GREATLY LOVED

There is no doubt that Rachel was the love of Jacob's life. Dr. George Matheson, in his comparison of Leah and Rachel, comments, "I should say that Leah had the keys of Jacob's house; Rachel the keys to Jacob's heart. Leah seems to have influenced his judgment; Rachel never ceased to hold his love."[9] The record says that *"Jacob loved Rachel"* (Genesis 29:18). She was the best loved, for she was the first and the fairest to be seen. We have Jacob's pronouncement, *"Ye know that my wife bare me two sons"* (Genesis 44:27). *"My wife"*—no mention of Leah and her large brood of children. Those two sons of Rachel's, Joseph and Benjamin, were love-children. The deep, mutual love of Jacob and Rachel found fulfillment in these sons. Another evidence of the love Jacob bore for Rachel is in the pathetic phrase *"Rachel died by me"* (Genesis 48:7), or, as another expresses it, *"To my sorrow Rachel died"* (verse 7 ESV). What a sorrowful allusion to a parting he could not forget! Whenever he thought of her passing, emotion was kindled within his empty heart. "The grave of Rachel remained ever green in the heart of Jacob, and he never ceased in fancy to deck it with flowers."[10] Joseph was also moved with the same deep feeling as an aged father when he referred to his mother, the parting from whom he never forgot.

But the most remarkable proof of Jacob's love for Rachel is suggested by the phrases *"Jacob served seven years for Rachel; and they seemed unto him but a few days, for the love he had to her"* (Genesis 29:20) and "[Jacob] *served...seven other years"* (Genesis 29:30; see also verse 27). He served Laban fourteen years in all

---

9. George Matheson, *Portraits of Bible Women.*
10. Ibid.

for Rachel. How he must have loved her to work so long! As we know, this was occasioned by Laban's deception in substituting Leah for Rachel. Evidently, he was not pleased that Rachel was preferred to the elder Leah, and he perhaps felt that the plainer daughter would be left on his hands. What a shock it must have been for Jacob to find that he had been cruelly beguiled by Laban! Did he hear in the deception the reverberation of his own sin? Having been guilty of deceiving his own father and brother, he found himself reaping what he had sown as the husband of two wives.

Yet, in spite of such a polygamous entanglement, Rachel was always first in the mind of her lover, even after her lamented death. Does not the unchanging love Jacob had for Rachel suggest a higher relationship? Are we the Lord's? Then He loves us best of all. He loves us better than any other part of His creation—better than the brown cornfields, lovely landscapes, glorious sunsets, majestic seas, silvery rivers, rippling lakes, starry heavens, beautiful birds, and other masterpieces of His handiwork. He never shed His tears over them or His blood for them. God loves us better than archangels or cherubim and seraphim. His beloved Son served for us as Jacob did for Rachel, and He loves us with a deeper, truer love than human love. He served for us not fourteen years but a lifetime. He toiled, endured, and suffered all through those thirty-three years, then bled and died in shame and nakedness on a wooden gibbet. *"Christ also loved the church, and gave himself for it"* (Ephesians 5:25). What a royal example! Souls are won for Him only by those who share Calvary's love and compassion for them.

RACHEL WAS BEAUTIFUL

Of the two daughters of Laban, we read, *"Leah was tender eyed; but Rachel was beautiful and well favoured"* (Genesis 29:17). Rachel had a beauty of form and features, giving her a compelling attractiveness, which captivated Jacob's heart. The Hebrew suggests "beautiful in form and beautiful in look." Her name means "the ewe," an animal known for its grace and loveliness. *Leah*, on the other hand, means "languor, weariness," probably because of her droopy look. *"Tender eyed"* implies dull, bleary eyes, possibly due to some form of ophthalmia common to the hot, sandy region where she lived. Ellicott's comment is helpful: "Leah's blurred eyes would be regarded in the East as a great defect, just as bright eyes were much admired." (See 1 Samuel 16:12, where David is described as *"goodly to look to"* [in Hebrew, "fair of eyes"].) Yet it was not Rachel—with her fair face and well-proportioned figure, object of her husband's lasting love—who was the mother of the progenitor of the Messiah, but the "weary-eyed Leah."

Rachel, with all the beauty of her aunt Rebekah, immediately possessed Jacob, who was dazzled by her loveliness because of the poetic aspect of his own nature. Watching Rachel as she drew water for the flocks, Jacob's eyes feasted upon her attractiveness and her charm of movement, and immediately he fell in love with her. At that moment, the red heat of affection was generated in his heart, and its warmth and glow remained throughout their years together.

In ourselves we are like Leah, plain and unattractive, with the eyes of our soul bleared by sin. But in Christ, we are as Rachel, *"beautiful and well favoured"* (Genesis 29:17), or, as the female Solomon depicts, *"black, but comely"* (Song of Solomon 1:5). In ourselves we are ugly, unfavorable, and distorted. *"In* [us] *(that is, in* [our] *flesh,) dwelleth no good thing"* (Romans 7:18);

but, clad in His grace, beauty, and righteousness, we are all fair. How blessed to know that God sees us in His beloved Son, and that we are accepted in Him, seeing we are covered with His robe of righteousness! (See Ephesians 1:6; Isaiah 61:10.) The beauty of the Lord our God is upon us.

Thou hast bid me gaze upon Thee,
And Thy beauty fills my soul,
For by Thy transforming power,
Thou hast made me whole.[11]

RACHEL WAS BARREN

An Oriental proverb assumes that a childless wife is as good as dead, and likely this is the meaning of Rachel's heartbroken cry, "*Give me children, or else I die*" (Genesis 30:1). Among Hebrew women, it was counted a great affliction to go through life sterile and childless. How heart-moving is the vow of childless Hannah: "*Look on the affliction of thine handmaid, and remember me*" (1 Samuel 1:11)! Graciously the Lord did look upon her affliction of barrenness and bless her with a son who became the first of the great prophets in the prophetic school of the Old Testament. And here is Rachel's similar request. Oh, the sorrow of it. She was beautiful but barren—favored but fruitless!

Is there not a spiritual truth for our hearts in Rachel's plight? Are we not barren insofar as bringing sinners to a spiritual birth is concerned? The beauty of the Lord is upon us, but we are fruitless. We have a name that we live but are dead—dead in respect to the Holy Spirit's activity and vitality in our lives, and dead in respect to success in service. If we do not maintain deep love for the Lord and for His Word, we will not have a passion

11. Jean Sophia Pigott, "Jesus, I Am Resting, Resting," 1876.

to bear souls or to rescue sinners. Are we saved but sterile? How tragic that many have been the Lord's for years yet, through the whole of their Christian life, have failed to lead a soul to Him! We have beautiful churches, an educated ministry, interesting sermons—but no children coming to birth. The womb of profession and witness is not producing those born of the Spirit. People are added to churches as members who, in the majority of cases, have never experienced the throes of a spiritual birth. We know so little of the apostolic travailing in birth until Christ is formed in the hearts of the lost.

RACHEL WEPT

It would seem as if there were three reasons why Rachel longed and wept to be saved from her barrenness. Rachel wept that she might emulate her sister, Leah, for we read that *"Rachel envied her sister"* (Genesis 30:1).

As she watched Leah's brood of children increase, Rachel's yearning to bear children for Jacob became more intense. The abounding fruitfulness of her sister stirred up covetous feelings in her disappointed heart. Cannot we draw a lesson from this desire to emulate Leah in childbearing? Are we possessed with a holy, legitimate covetousness? We have every right to win souls, and in the plan of God, every believer should be a soulwinner. No preacher or evangelist has a monopoly on soulwinning. Each of us has the commission to make disciples.

God seeks to use *you* as much as He uses anyone else, if not more so. You must not let others outstrip you when it comes to soulwinning. Since Pentecost, many have been mightily blessed of the Spirit in spiritual births. Peter and the three thousand saved on the historic day of Pentecost; Paul and the multitude he brought to Christ; John Knox; John Wesley; George Whitefield;

David Brainerd; D. L. Moody; and a host of others have cried, "Give me children, or else we die," and God made them mighty in the salvation of sinners. As we think of others who have borne many spiritual children, conspicuous or otherwise, do we envy them and seek to eliminate anything in our lives that would make it difficult for God to reach others through us?

Later on, Rachel says, "*With great wrestlings have I wrestled with my sister, and I have prevailed*" (Genesis 30:8). This marks intensity and passion—a mighty, prevailing intercession. For those wrestlings were not in rivalry with Leah but "the wrestlings of God." The phrase "*great wrestlings*" means "the wrestlings of El," or "mighty wrestlings with God in prayer." Without such passion, we cannot prevail. If we would bless, we must bleed. Our spiritual sterility will never depart unless there is Spirit-inspired intercession. Jeremiah could write, "*Mine eye runneth down with rivers of water for the destruction of the daughter of my people. Mine eye trickleth down, and ceaseth not, without any intermission*" (Lamentations 3:48–49). No wonder they called him the "weeping prophet"! Jesus beheld the city of Jerusalem and wept (see Luke 19:41–42), and the shedding of His tears for His rejecters led to the shedding of His blood to save them.

O for a passionate passion for souls!
O for a pity that yearns!
O for a love that loves unto death!
O for the fire that burns!
O for the pure prayer-power that prevails,
That pours itself out for the lost;
Victorious prayer in the Conqueror's name,
O for a Pentecost![12]

12. Amy Carmichael, "A Passion for Souls."

BECOMING DEARER TO HER HUSBAND

Rachel had a fear that her continued barrenness might cause Jacob to despise her. She longed for their love-union to be blessed with a child, forging a closer link between them. As much as she loved Jacob, she knew that bearing children would produce a still deeper attachment to each other. Here is another feature of Rachel's cry that we can apply to ourselves as professed lovers of the Lord. If we desire to become more precious to our heavenly Husband, even our blessed Lord Jesus, then we must have a deep and ever-deepening love for the perishing. When He hears us making Rachel's request our own, "Give me children, or else I die," then we will become dearer to His heart, and He will embrace us more firmly. When we plead, toil, suffer, and weep for souls, we but reflect Calvary's compassion for a lost world, and our intercession for souls becomes an echo of Christ's own intense cry.

SHARING THE HOPE OF BECOMING AN ANCESTRESS OF THE MESSIAH

Every Hebrew woman was dominated by the desire to produce the promised Seed. (See Genesis 3:15.) The covenant God had made to Abraham brought hope to every loyal feminine heart that the Messiah might come through her. In his salutation to Mary, Gabriel said, *"Blessed art thou among women"* (Luke 1:28). All God-fearing women had longed for the privilege of bringing the Promised One into the world. The poor but godly peasant girl Mary was the divinely chosen one to become the mother of our Lord.

As every Hebrew woman longed to be the chosen vessel for the fulfillment of God's purpose, so we must yearn to be used in causing Christ to be formed in those who know Him not. Furthermore, every soul we win for Him brings nearer the completion of His body, the church, and His second coming. Are we reproducing the image of the Lord in others' lives, thereby hastening His glorious appearing? It avails nothing for a person that Christ was born in Bethlehem if He has not been born in his heart by faith. We must humbly confess that we know so little of what it means to travail in birth until Christ is born as Savior in those who are strangers to grace.

RACHEL BECAME FRUITFUL

Rachel's tears ended in triumph; her heartfelt cry resulted in conquest—"*Rachel had born Joseph*" (Genesis 30:25); "*the sons of Rachel; Joseph, and Benjamin*" (Genesis 35:24). Said the well-wishers of Ruth when she bore Obed, and thus became the ancestress of our Lord, "*The Lord make* [thee] *like Rachel and like Leah, which two did build the house of Israel*" (Ruth 4:11). At last, Rachel's longing was appeased and her heart ravished as she held her baby Joseph in her arms. Her barrenness was ended, her husband was satisfied, and God was glorified. For her, the promise was fulfilled: "*Sing, O barren, thou that didst not bear*" (Isaiah 54:1). How Rachel must have rejoiced over her precious gift of a son—and what a famous son he became in Israel's history! Truly, he was a child worth waiting for.

A fruitless Christian life—what a blight it is! How dishonoring it is to the Lord of life, as well as disastrous to ourselves! Yet no matter how barren we have been, having never won a single soul for Christ, we can become fruitful. We can go forth "unctionized" by the Holy Spirit, functioning as mighty soul-winners. He who brings souls to spiritual birth can make us like Rachel and Leah—builders of the house of the Lord, even His mystical body. May grace be ours to confess our lack of passion, zeal, intensity, heartache, and soul-travail for the lost! May we determine to put away all known hindrances and strained relationships! May we get right with God and with others and thus be fit and ready for Him to use! When Rachel left home, she took with her the gods of Laban's home (see Genesis 31:19–20, 34), which implied that she had tried to serve God *and* her idols. We must tear any idol from the throne of our heart, and enthrone God as the Lord Supreme. Then we can go out as effective winners of souls. If we would be neither barren nor unfruitful, then we must manifest the virtues Peter reminds us of. (See 2 Peter 1:4–8.)

Further, if we desire to be used in the salvation of souls, we must be willing for God to lead and guide us into right avenues of service. Rachel's name, as we have seen, means "the ewe," and is from a word signifying "to be gentle." Perhaps the name was suggestive of Rachel's disposition. If we would follow the Lamb wherever He leads, then we must be lamblike, or gentle—kind and loving in our approach to those we seek to reach for the Savior. We must be winsome if we would "win some" for Him. Whether we be pastor, preacher, or worker, our preeminent task is that of rescuing the perishing. At the judgment seat, we shall be judged not by our scholarship but by souls won for Christ; not by our eloquence but by our entreaty; not by our preaching but by our passion; not by our writings but by our wrestlings; not by our ability to raise money and build churches or to draw and influence crowds but by the power we expended to agonize men and women into the kingdom of God. Without the cry of Rachel continually prominent in any church, it is but a well-dressed corpse. Its architecture, music, and order of service may be attractive; but, so far as God is concerned, such a church is dead. Christ builds His church by using her to win the souls He can make as *"lively stones"* (1 Peter 2:5) to complete such a mystic fabric. The first and paramount obligation, then, of any church or Christian is to pluck souls out of the fire. (See Jude 23.)

RACHEL DIED IN TRAVAIL

What a moving spectacle we have in the record of Rachel's painful death in childbirth!

> *And they journeyed from Bethel; and there was but a little way to come to Ephrath: and Rachel travailed, and she had hard labour. And it came to pass, when she was in hard labour, that the midwife said unto her, Fear not; thou shalt have this son also. And it came to pass, as her soul was in departing, (for she died) that she called his name Benoni: but his father called him Benjamin.* (Genesis 35:16–18)

She passed out of her sorrow and pain near Bethlehem, and her heartbroken husband buried her there and erected a pillar over her grave. (See Genesis 35:19–20; 1 Samuel 10:2.) To his mother, who died bringing him to birth, the child was Benoni, son of sorrow; but to his father, he was Benjamin, meaning "son of my right hand." Benjamin became the one especially honored among the Gentiles. (See Genesis 45:22.)

In this tragic episode, death and life throes meet. A mother goes down to death in giving life to a child. We can gather the following two thoughts from this sorrowful scene.

DEATH LEADS TO LIFE

Rachel dies, but Benjamin is born; and so life springs from death. Our Lord taught that unless the corn of wheat dies, it cannot bring forth fruit. (See John 12:24.) Such an illustration was a foregleam of the cross. Fairer and more beautiful than Rachel, Jesus died at Calvary; and out of His death, countless myriads have been spiritually born. In their salvation, He sees of the travail of His soul and is satisfied. How slow we are to learn that life can spring only from death, that we cannot win the lost unless we die to self with all its wretched forms of ease, indulgence, and self-glory! It is only as we "lay in dust life's glory dead" that there can rise from the ground "life that shall endless be."[13] Are we willing to "die daily," that others might be brought to life?

RACHEL DIED IN ANGUISH AT EPHRATH

This beautiful woman died in Ephrath, which means "fruitful," as she bore another son. Thus would I live, and thus would I die, winning and saving precious souls! If I should go home to heaven by the way of a grave, I pray that I may be privileged to die pleading with God for souls and pleading with souls for God. Countless numbers have been born anew by the Spirit through the dying, triumphant witness of the saints of God. Saul of Tarsus watched Stephen die a terrible yet victorious death, and he was never the same man again. May we be found burning out for God—consumed with an undying passion to win others! The church's deepest need today is for those who live for souls, plead for souls, yearn for souls, and die for souls to concentrate every breath, word, thought, and action upon this supreme service.

Because the sands of time are sinking, it is incumbent upon each of us to make Rachel's cry our daily prayer—"O Lord, give me children, or else I die." (See Genesis 30:1.) We must not shrink from travail-pains, for when Zion travailed, she brought forth. Bringing Benjamin to birth is most costly but wonderfully rewarding. Let us not forget, then, that in the plan of God, every believer should be a soulwinner. Bringing men to Christ is not the prerogative of professional evangelists. A church in which every member seeks to win others for the Savior has no need of an evangelist. May God help us to...

13. George Matheson, "O Love That Wilt Not Let Me Go," 1882.

Seek the coming of His kingdom;
Seek the souls around, to win them,
Seek to Jesus Christ to bring them:
Seek this first, seek this first.[14]

14. Georgiana M. Taylor, "Seek Ye First, Not Earthly Pleasure."

CHAPTER FOUR

ELIJAH: THE PROPHET WHO WAS CONSPICUOUS FOR HIS SOLITUDE

As the Bible is largely biographical, it carries an irresistible charm for our hearts, seeing that the characters portrayed therein reflect human nature in every age. Within its portrait gallery, we find those who experienced trials and triumphs similar to those we face in the twentieth century. We now consider another of its unforgettable personalities—the strong and rugged prophet of the desert, Elijah the Tishbite, who, in some respects, is the greatest of the prophets in the Old Testament. So great was he that we can approach his remarkable life from different angles, all of which are profitable for our own spiritual life. We choose to concentrate, however, on the most outstanding fact of his career—his *solitude*. Percy Bysshe Shelley wrote of loving "tranquil solitude," but Elijah's solitude was not always of the tranquil kind.

Had we the space, we could dwell upon the following features of the life of this miracle-working prophet:

- Elijah has been twice upon the earth, and if (as some prophetic students affirm) he may be one of the two witnesses John speaks of, then he will come back to earth again. (See Matthew 17:3–4; Revelation 11:3.)
- Elijah was a man who never tasted death. Like Enoch, his body was never buried in a grave. If he is to return to earth as one of the two witnesses, he will be slain; and, along with his companion martyr, his dead body will lie in the street. (See Revelation 11:8.) Elijah accompanied a man born some one thousand years before him, namely, Moses, when he came down from heaven to the Mount of Transfiguration to speak with Jesus about His death at Calvary.
- Elijah, like Enoch, experienced miraculous translation. Although these two worthies were not able to sing, "Oh, joy! Oh, delight! should we go without dying,"[15] both of them knew what it was to be caught up to meet the Lord.
- Elijah, under God, had power over two of the greatest elements in nature—fire and water. He could bring fire down and keep the water up.
- Elijah was a miracle-worker, as his many miracles in various realms prove. He knew that, of himself, he had no might, but that his power was of God.
- Elijah was a man who, in spite of his grandeur and greatness and mighty works and preaching, was a man of like passions as ourselves.

However, the commanding feature of his sojourn on earth was his solitude. Above all else, Elijah was the man who experienced "the self-sufficing power of solitude," as Wordsworth put it. Perhaps no other Bible saint lived a more lonely life than this prophet whose career was one of aloneness and aloofness.

---

15. H. L. Turner, "Christ Returneth," 1878.

Because of his sensational, dramatic, and miraculous experiences, unshared by others, Elijah stands out as a man shut off from men but shut up with God.

This stern, righteous stalwart for God was essentially a man of the desert. He stepped abruptly upon the stage by divine plan, coming from some quiet country, some rural sphere, and he remained a man of the open spaces. Like many other champions God raised up out of obscurity for a conspicuous ministry, Elijah was a nobody who became a somebody. God called Moses from the back side of the desert, David from the sheepfold, John the Baptist from the wilderness, and Jesus from His quiet country home.

Elijah owed his prominent position as a prophet not to his high birth or station, or to a native place of renown, or to his courage. He was born in Tishbe, probably a mean and obscure village among the mountains, to a poor, banished Jewish family. We have no record of his parentage and early life. It would seem as if he knew nothing of schools of learning and worldly grandeur, which men court and count as necessary to securing a position in the world. God has often delighted to choose the weak things of the world to confound the mighty (see 1 Corinthians 1:27), to prove that His choice is not of flesh and blood. This prophet bears the title "Elijah the Tishbite"—*Tishbite* meaning "converter." And the name befits his life and labors, for under God, he was the means of reclaiming multitudes out of the dark idolatry and apostasy of his time.

ALONE WITH HEAVEN: DEPENDENCE

Elijah did not live in a little world all his own. William Cowper wrote, "How sweet, how passing sweet, is solitude." And the prophet's solitude was sweet because it was shared by

God: "*The Lord God of Israel...before whom I stand*" (1 Kings 17:1). The secret, then, of his remarkable power was his aloneness with God; for in the divine Presence, he allowed God to search, penetrate, and command him. Communion with God in the desert was the sublime secret of Elijah's spiritual character. Ever conscious that he was nothing in himself, he could yet seek divine authority and power to open and shut the heavens, raise the dead, cause the living to die, and bring judgment upon the enemies of God.

The name of this unique man is suggestive, for Elijah means "my God of power," or "Jehovah is my strength." Such an excellent name must have been chosen by godly parents. He lived out its meaning in deed and in truth. Like you and me, he was nothing in himself but invincible when girded by divine strength. Of himself, Elijah could do nothing, yet deeds of omnipotence proceeded from his hands because, in his solitude, he had traffic with heaven. In "A Poet's Epitaph," Wordsworth has a couplet we can apply to Elijah the prophet:

> And impulses of deeper birth
> Have come to him in solitude.

ALONE AT THE BROOK: DEARTH

> *The word of the Lord came unto* [Elijah], *saying, Get thee hence, and turn thee eastward, and hide thyself by the brook Cherith, that is before Jordan. And it shall be, that thou shalt drink of the brook; and I have commanded the ravens to feed thee there. So he went and did according unto the word of the Lord: for he went and dwelt by the brook Cherith, that is before Jordan. And the ravens brought him bread and flesh in the morning, and bread and flesh in the evening; and he drank of the brook.* (1 Kings 17:2–6)

According to Elijah's divinely inspired command, the heavens closed and became as brass, the fountains failed, and the brooks dried up. The sun shone fiercely upon the earth, burning all verdure by its scorching beams—a symbol of the eyes of the Lord as a flame of fire destroying man for his gross iniquity. Every day, Elijah saw the famine of food and water approach, and he wondered whether he was to share in the common calamity pronounced upon the guilty nation. Then came the command to go to the brook at Cherith, where God said He would take care of the fearless prophet and feed him in unaccustomed ways. The prophet was indeed a man of faith—he could stand alone when his sustenance was cut off, and trust God absolutely and entirely to meet his every need. This is where Elimelech failed. He forgot the promise of Psalm 37:19: *"In the days of famine* [you] *shall be satisfied."*

Think of Elijah as he dwelled near the banks of Jordan where dead silence reigned, and no human footsteps were heard or seen in all that wild and solitary country. Yet here sat this man in his hairy mantle, reflecting on God and His ways. To quote Wordsworth again, "On Man, on Nature, and on Human Life, Musing in solitude."

When solitude seemed to weary him, and the surrounding rocks cave in upon him, faith and hope would be strengthened as he was shut in with God—a prisoner for His sake. For twelve months, he lived in the rocky vale at Cherith with no one to serve him but the ravens, those black livery waiters who came to the hungry prophet morning and night, laden with meat and bread. God is elsewhere pictured as feeding the ravens; here He uses these birds to feed His lonely servant. Few of us, I fear, know what it is to be alone in this respect, shut off from all sources of supply, and to experience that God, with His magnificent omnipotence, is able to meet all our need. How wonderful He is at spreading a table in the wilderness!

ALONE WITH A POOR WIDOW: DESTITUTION

Because Elijah believed that "solitude is the mother-country of the strong,"[16] he was a man ready for any crisis or emergency. A good servant obeys the moment the bell rings; and when God called the prophet to go out to an almost impossible task, he went. Without question or demur, he fulfilled the divine will, although at times what was asked seemed to be contrary to the accustomed order of things. Elijah was ready for sacrifice or service, pain or poverty, suffering or success, trial or triumph. The solitary prophet, like his New Testament counterpart, John the Baptist, stood clothed in camel's hair, unafraid of the face of man, and ready to do God's will.

Destitution is a terrible test of faith. It requires plenty and prosperity to keep some people contented as well as consecrated. If you have an innate passion for independence, how would you like to be beggared of all and made dependent upon the scanty provision of a poor widow woman? But Elijah's greatness was of such quality that he was able to go into this phase of solitude and, alone with a widow, prove that God was able to feed him in a destitute home, just as He had done by the ravens at the brook. At Zarephath, Elijah proved that the barrel of meal wasted not, and the cruse of oil did not fail. When the barrel was almost empty, God heard the scraping at the bottom and provided a fresh supply. (See 1 Kings 17:8–16.) *And the God of Elijah still lives.*

ALONE WITH THE DEAD: DEATH

What a poignant scene for some artist to depict is the house of mourning the historian describes in 1 Kings 17:17–24! The

16. Alexander Maclaren, *The Wearied Christ.*

bereaved widow is bowed down with grief as she sits with her dead child clasped to her heart, her face bathed with tears over both her dead son and her sins. But Elijah, so grateful to this woman at Zarephath for her care of him, and sure that God was able to raise up the child, takes the corpse from the mother's arms and goes upstairs to his own small chamber, to which he often retired for prayer and meditation. Closing the door, Elijah falls to his knees to pour out his heart before God. There is the prophet, alone with the dead! Perhaps this was the climax of his loneliness. In describing such a lonely experience, John Keats wrote:

> A solitary sorrow best befits
> Thy lips, and antheming a lonely grief.[17]

Who can express the solitary grief of a crushed heart when alone with the dead before burial? But the solitary sorrow of the weeping widow and the lonely grief of Elijah soon vanished, for God heard the voice of the prophet pleading for the dead child, and He restored him to life. Carrying the boy downstairs to his sorrowful mother, Elijah uttered the joyful news: "*Thy son liveth*" (1 Kings 17:23). Such a miracle confirmed Elijah as a man of God and as a faithful messenger of truth.

For those of us whose supreme task is that of soulwinning, how urgent it is to carry into the presence of God those who are spiritually dead among our relatives and friends and among the masses at home and abroad, to plead in agony over them until we see them rise again in newness of life. Eternity alone will reveal how many were brought to a spiritual resurrection because of those who, in the solitude of their prayer chamber, continued in intercession until those they held up to God were raised from their grave of iniquity. God's choicest wreaths are often wet with tears of intense intercession. (See Hebrews 5:7.)

---

17. John Keats, *Hyperion*.

Tho' sown in tears through weary years,
The seed will surely live;
Tho' great the cost, it is not lost,
For God will fruitage give.[18]

ALONE WITH AHAB: DEFIANCE

Elijah was the most uncompromising of men. Bribery did not tempt this bold man, whose iron will knew no yielding to expediency. At times, it may seem as if he was hard in his holiness; but although he manifested severity, he was a stranger to temerity and trickery. How his character throws into relief these loose, vacillating, compromising men in our decadent days when equity has fallen on the streets! The righteousness of this lionhearted prophet is as a plummet. What unflinching loyalty to the God of truth and to the truth of God were his as he confronted Ahab, son of Omri, who did evil in the sight of Jehovah above all who were before him!

No true man of God can escape a feeling of loneliness as he stands before a person he does not like because of his wrongdoing and sin. It is human nature to follow the crowd, to go with the tide. But it is godlike to stand alone in defiance of Satan and his works. Yet defiance without dependency on God is fruitless, for it has no inner strength. If we know how to live alone with the God of power, then we will not fear as we seek to rebuke the world's mad strife.

Ahab was a man of sin who had set up the satanic trinity of the calf, Baal, and Ashera—the most awful of the three. Against this dark background of idolatry, Elijah the fearless prophet is displayed. Gloomy idols and temples rose on every hand; profane altars stained with the blood of holy men were common;

18. Jessie Brown Pounds, "Seeds of Promise."

and an arrogant defiance of the Most High God called for divine vengeance. It seemed as if Satan had transferred his residence from hell to earth and strove to obscure the light of heaven by the smoke and vapor of the most horrible forms of idolatry. But amid it all, the defiant figure of Elijah the Tishbite poured out denunciations upon the profligates until they trembled beneath his terrible words.

What our idolatrous world needs is an Elijah on every Mount Carmel, a John the Baptist in every Herod's court, an apostle John on every Isle of Patmos, and a John Knox in every pulpit, to expose and defy the rulers of the darkness of this age.

Many mighty men are lost
Daring not to stand,
Who for God had been a host
By joining Daniel's band.[19]

There are two occasions when Elijah heard God issuing instructions, and the first seems to contradict the second: *"Hide thyself"* (1 Kings 17:3) and *"Go, shew thyself"* (1 Kings 18:1). Let us note the significance of these two commands and the connection between them.

"HIDE THYSELF BY THE BROOK"

The various phases of aloneness we have already considered form a fitting commentary on this stem word Elijah heard God utter. It teaches us that privacy must precede publicity, that solitude determines our power in society, and that aloneness is essential to activity. We live too much in the company of others—we need more of the hidden, solitary life. It was only when Daniel was alone with God that he received His secrets, and such a law operates throughout Scripture. *"I was*

19. Philip P. Bliss, "Dare to Be a Daniel," 1873.

left alone, and saw this great vision" (Daniel 10:8). God must have His Josephs in prisons before He can place them in palaces, His Abrahams alone with Himself before He can make great nations of them, His Daniels cast into a den of lions before they can move with royalty in Babylon, and His Pauls left as dead before they can stand before kings and rulers to testify of His grace. Our blessed Lord Himself spent thirty obscure years in the village of Nazareth before His brief but dynamic ministry, which gave birth to Christianity. Often during His public appearance, "He departed to a solitary place and prayed." (See Mark 1:35.)

God's *"Hide thyself"* is equivalent to the Master's *"Come ye…apart"* (Mark 6:31). We need more of the shut door, for in spiritual photography, the darkroom is the fitting place for the development of the image of God on life and in service. Jesus "trod the winepress alone." (See Isaiah 63:3.) God's command for Elijah to hide himself was necessary for the prophet's well-being at that stage in his career. The victory to come when he stood before Ahab demanded that he be called apart to isolation and separation to store his spiritual battery with power to call down fire from heaven. Only as we come apart from the world to make contact with heaven can we go into all the world and preach the converting gospel.

Go hide thyself ere Carmel's triumph come,
A deeper life in Him we all must know.
We must all come apart with Christ alone
Ere He can use us, He must keep us low—
Go *hide* thyself.

GO, SHEW THYSELF UNTO TO AHAB

When we allow privacy to do its perfect work, then we are ready for the public service God has prepared for us. In his solitude at Cherith, Elijah had access to God through opened heavens, but see what happened as he came from his hiding place. Mantled by God, he made the heavens as brass and the earth as iron. Essential to both man and beast, dew and rain were restrained. The word of the prophet struck like a fever in the heart of the earth, withering and scorching all that was fresh and green. Streams and rivulets dried up, and all that had breath languished for the space of three and a half years. Such miraculous, disastrous effects were produced by the voice of a man who in loneliness was a man in accord with the Almighty, hearing only His commanding voice. Having power with God, Elijah prevailed.

There is a time to leave solitude and stand before society, to go from the closet to the crowd and declare publicly what God has revealed in private. May we be saved from the folly of trying to speak to Ahab before speaking to the Almighty, and from standing before others without first standing before Him. John the Baptist, we read, remained in the deserts until his showing unto Israel—and what a "showing" it was because of the training of the dreary desert with its solitude! When God says, "Go, show thyself," then we can go and run through a troop of difficulties and leap over the wall of seeming impossibilities. After those days away from the world, spent in the upper room praying, the disciples went forth to a mighty Pentecost and became ambassadors with power and authority as they proclaimed the Evangel of grace. They became invincible messengers of the invincible God and earthen vessels filled with heavenly treasure. May we learn to hide ourselves when God says, "Hide thyself," and to show ourselves as His sent ones when He says, "Go, show thyself"!

Go show thyself ere Carmel's triumph come,
The drying brook of Cherith wrought the power.

The soul that waits alone upon its God
Is fitted for His use in danger's hour.
Go show thyself.

ALONE WITH HIMSELF: DISGUST

After Elijah's courageous defiance of King Ahab and the marvelous display of divine power on Mount Carmel, he wilted before the blatant taunt of Jezebel to slay him even as he had slaughtered her godless prophets. (See 1 Kings 19:1–7.) Elijah stood bravely before the king; he unashamedly "showed himself." But he ran away from a woman and lost himself once more in the solitude of the desert. The conflict on Carmel had been a great strain on Elijah; it exacted a physical toll of even his strong, rugged frame. The torch was badly shaken, but afterward, it glowed brighter.

How pathetic it is to see this strong, courageous man sitting under a juniper tree like an exile in fearful solitude, wishing he might die! Alone with himself, he was filled with disgust and contempt, as Job was when he said, *"I am vile"* (Job 40:4), and Isaiah also when he cried, "I am unclean." (See Isaiah 6:5.) Elijah said, *"Take away my life; for I am not better than my fathers"* (1 Kings 19:4). If, at any time, we feel despised and sigh because of the burdens and trials of life, let us not flee, as Elijah did, and sit under a juniper tree thinking all is lost; but let us sit before another tree where the incarnate Son of God was made a curse for us, and there find refreshment for our weary, distracted spirits. God understood all about the reaction of His faithful prophet, and He took tender care of him, even to sending an angel to prepare the overwrought challenger of Ahab a most hearty meal.

A person wonders if Elijah would have been so lonely a man if he had had a dear companion to turn to in the hour of physical strain. It was Bacon who expressed the sentiment, "The worst solitude is to be destitute of sincere friendship." As there is no mention of Elijah's wife, the inference is that he did not have such a close companion to turn to for comfort. It is not without significance that after Elijah's flight from Jezebel when he was filled with despair, God raised up for him a close friend—Elisha, his successor—who never left the prophet's side until the end of his service.

ALONE IN A CAVE: DEFEAT

From his feelings of despair, Elijah went on to defeatism. "*I, even I only, am left*" (1 Kings 19:10). After a journey of forty days, this solitary traveler came to Mount Horeb and took up his abode in a cave where God's ways with him led to further self-mortification and self-denial. Here we see the man of God in circumstances overruled to increase his humility and the expression of the life of God in his soul. Silently and mournfully he contemplates the decay of his last and fondest hope. Then, out of the deep silence of his solitary abode, a loving voice reaches his ear: "*What doest thou here, Elijah?*" (1 Kings 19:13).

The prophet was to learn that his was a defeat spelling victory, for when God gets us to the end of ourselves, He is ready to show us His beginnings. Elijah had been conspicuous as an agent of fire and thunder, but in the divine unfolding, he came to learn that grace alone can soften, melt, and convert the heart. He received the revelation that the results he anticipated from the thunders of the law and the divine judgments could come only through the loving-kindness and tender mercy of Jehovah.

Following the *"Hide thyself"* (1 Kings 17:3) and the *"Go, shew thyself"* (1 Kings 18:1) came the *"Go, return on thy way to the wilderness"* (1 Kings 19:15). And forth from the lonely cave he went to fulfill a divine commission. John Greenleaf Whittier has the wonderful verse,

O Sabbath rest by Galilee,
O calm of hills above,
Where Jesus knelt to share with Thee
The silence of eternity,
Interpreted by love![20]

In the calm of that cave, Elijah came to share with God "the silence of eternity," and to understand its loving interpretation by the *"still, small voice"* (1 Kings 19:12).

ALONE AT THE END: DELIGHT

The sons of the prophets had a foreboding that the end of Elijah was near, and they expressed their fear to him, who told them to say nothing about such a somber event. There was, however, no need for them to be quiet about the matter, seeing that Elijah knew that the closing scene of his life was at hand. Further, no matter in what form his end was to come, he wanted to meet it even as he had lived—alone. But Elisha was bound by an oath not to leave his master; so we have the dramatic episode of Elijah dividing Jordan with his mantle, and, like Israel before them, they went over on dry ground. Elijah requested Elisha to ask for a parting gift: *"Ask what I shall do for thee, before I be taken away from thee"* (2 Kings 2:9). All that Elisha desired was for a double portion of his remarkable master's spirit to rest upon him, which was granted, for he performed twice as many miracles as Elijah.

20. John Greenleaf Whittier, "Dear Lord and Father of Mankind," 1872.

The day dawned when the Lord was to take Elijah up to heaven by a whirlwind. What a fitting exit for a man who had had a whirlwind career! Chariots of fire and horses of fire appeared and parted the two prophets, and Elijah's solitude was thus terminated by a whirlwind translation to heaven, where he would be solitary no more. But does he not remain a pattern for your life and mine? As he was a man of like passions as ourselves, his experiences teach us that spiritual solitude is better in every way than the society of the world. His entrance into history was like his entrance into heaven—dramatic. And our end may be as his.

Elijah did not go to glory by the usual way of the grave. Like Enoch before him, *"he was not; for God took him"* (Genesis 5:24). He had the delight of being caught up without dying, and God took him, in his old, wrinkled, desert-hardened body, to Himself. The wonder is that he appeared with it again, glorified, when he came down from heaven with Moses to meet Jesus on the mount. The blessed hope is that if Jesus should return today, as He may, our translation would be as sudden and dramatic as Elijah's, even though ours will not be with the accompanying chariots and horses of fire. We are to be caught up in clouds of believers—a vast translation host of the redeemed from every nation—to meet the Lord in the air, and then to be with Him where He dwells forever.

CHAPTER FIVE

Saul: The King Who Forsook God for a Witch

One sign of the reality and truthfulness of Scripture is that it sets up as beacons of warning not only those whose lives were conspicuously bad but persons in whom there was a conflict between good and evil, with evil ultimately prevailing. Men who were entrusted with high privileges and responsibilities fell back into a baser life, despising their loftier calling. Thus it was with Saul, Israel's first king, whose true character is brought out by various experiences in his life. This son of Kish is an outstanding example of those Bible characters whose faults appear greater when contrasted with those of the noble characters who surrounded them.

Saul had close contact with the prophet Samuel, the man of prayer. If only he had prayed as Samuel did, what a different story would have been his! David, the young champion Saul was so jealous of, was a man after God's own heart. (See 1 Samuel 13:14; Acts 13:22.) If only Saul had been as noble, true, and God-fearing as the son of Jesse, what lapses of faith and obedience he would have been spared. Jonathan, Saul's son, was a most lovely character. Had the father emulated the largeness of heart and sweetness of temperament the son manifested, how loved he would have been. But when it comes to the roll call of the heroes of faith, Saul's contemporaries Samuel and David find honorable mention, while the king who ruled Israel for forty years is excluded from this chapter of remembrance. (See Hebrews 11:32.)

Saul's story is a tragic one of regression of soul. His life was made up of a series of gradual changes for the worse, evil always prevailing over the good. In many respects, he is the most pathetic character in the gallery of Old Testament men. His career began magnificently, but what unutterable pathos were expressed in its consummation! The warning is, "*Take heed lest* [ye] *fall*" (1 Corinthians 10:12). The son of Kish and a Benjamite (see 1 Samuel 9:1; 10:21), Saul, when he was anointed king, was "*a choice young man, and a goodly: and there was not among the children of Israel a goodlier person than he: from his shoulders and upward he was higher than any of the people*" (1 Samuel 9:2). If he had remained the "goodliest" person in Israel, what a worthy record would have been his. But "behold, how the mighty have fallen!" (See 2 Samuel 1:27.) The following episodes enable us to evaluate the virtues and vices of this king whom God chose but had to reject.

WITH THE DONKEYS

The first glimpse we have of this well-built young man of remarkable height is when he was out on the mountain seeking a drove of donkeys that had strayed from his father's farm at Gibeah. After a three-day circuit, he arrived at Zaph, where Samuel lived. Saul's servant advised him to consult the seer about the animals he could not find. A day before his visit, Samuel had received a divine intimation as to the approach of this striking Benjamite and of his future destiny as the king for which the people clamored. There is a precious thought in the phrase *"Now the Lord had told Samuel in his ear a day before Saul came"* (1 Samuel 9:15). The original text suggests the lifting up of the curls covering Samuel's ear and the Lord whispering His secret into it.

After Samuel and Saul met, the prophet revealed the plan of God; poured the consecrating oil on Saul's head; and, with a kiss of salutation, told Saul he was to be the ruler and deliverer of the nation. Though he still wore the garb of his domestic vocation, a highly privileged office was his.

Each stage of the return journey was marked by incidents confirming Samuel's predictions as to Saul's coming fortunes: As he passed the tomb of Rachel, the mother of Benjamin, of whom Saul was a descendant, he met two men who told him that the donkeys were safe but that his father was sorrowing, not for the animals but for Saul himself. Pursuing his journey, this newly anointed king had a vision of the tremendous work he had been called to do. How many there are who are born to be kings or to do great things for God but who spend their whole life in the pursuit of donkeys for want of some kind prophet to tell them that they are head and shoulders above others! It is interesting to note how many received a call to follow and serve God while they were busily engaged in secular vocations. Amos, for instance, was a herdsman and a gatherer of sycamore fruit when God came and took him from the flock to function as a prophet to Israel. (See Amos 7:14–15.)

AMONG THE PROPHETS

The first call—the private, inner call of his anointing as king—was thus far a secret known only to Samuel and Saul. There came another call when Saul met the prophets on the hill of God, from which he caught an inspiration of the loftier life, one he had never before conceived. The Holy Spirit came upon him, and he was given another heart. He received the fulfillment of promise "God is with thee." (See 1 Samuel 10:6, 10.) Saul came down from the mountain with his whole character changed as the result of such a noteworthy experience. This was equivalent to regeneration. Under the Spirit's power, he prophesied, which gave rise to the proverb *"Is Saul also among the prophets?"* (1 Samuel 10:11; 19:24). We learn from this episode that we can never achieve the plan of God for our lives unless we receive the divine endowment to accomplish it.

Saul had many natural qualities. When he commenced his reign, he was a stalwart, handsome, and attractive young man. He was also outstanding for his strength and activity; and because of his gigantic stature, he was a striking figure everyone looked to as he passed by. His beauty caused him to be "compared to the gazelle of Israel." In addition to his external appearance, he was chosen by God. *"See ye him whom the Lord hath chosen"* (1 Samuel 10:24). Over and above all his natural gifts and endowments, divine choice and equipment were necessary for him to succeed. You may be head and shoulders above others in respect to talents, gifts, and personality, but without a change of heart and the anointing with the Spirit, power will never be yours to reign in righteousness.

ON THE THRONE

The next crisis in Saul's transition from a farmer to a king took place at Mizpah, where Samuel had convened an assembly of the tribes of Israel. (See 1 Samuel 10:17–27.) There, lots were drawn to choose the king they demanded. The tribe of Benjamin came up trumps, and out of it the family of Matri was taken, and the lot fell upon Saul, the son of Kish. He was elected, but he could not be found. Then his hiding place was discovered, and Samuel presented him to the people with the acclamation, "*See ye him whom the Lord hath chosen, that there is none like him among all the people?*" (1 Samuel 10:24). Then, for the first time in Jewish history, the cry rent the air, "*God save the king!*" (verse 24). The national election was but the acceptance of a divine choice.

Up to this time, Saul had been a shy, retiring youth. "*Am not I a Benjamite…?*" (1 Samuel 9:21). Willingly, he would have retreated to private life, happy in the fields with his yoke of oxen. But, yielding to a divine and human choice, he gathered around him "*a band of men, whose hearts God had touched*" (1 Samuel 10:26) and led the people out to a remarkable victory over the Ammonites. Then, taking up his proper place as king, he became resolute and ruled with equity. For a while, Saul's reign was satisfactory and successful. In his cabinet was Samuel as chaplain, or spiritual adviser; Abner, his secretary of war; Abiathar, the high priest; and David, his lieutenant and confidential friend.

Among the high, kingly qualities Saul possessed were his reluctance to accept office, equaled only by the coolness with which he accepted it (see 1 Samuel 10:22; 11:5); the promptness with which he responded to the first call of duty (see 1 Samuel 11:6); and the lasting gratitude of the people of Jabesh-gilead for the timely aid he gave as king. Then, as Thomas Hunter Weir expresses it, "If we remember that Saul was openly disowned by Samuel (1 Samuel 15:30), and believed himself to be cast off by [Yahweh], we cannot but admire the way in which he fought on to the last. Moreover, the fact that he retained not only his own sons, but a sufficient body of fighting men to engage a large body of [Philistines], shows that there must have been something in him to excite confidence and loyalty."[21]

Chief among Saul's honorable and noble qualities as king were his prowess in war and his generosity in peace, which David, the man who knew him best, set down in his elegy. (See 2 Samuel 1:19.) There is no need to linger over all his exploits. Suffice it to say that gradually Saul gave way to passion and eccentric impulses. He became jealous, cruel, and vindictive. When he intruded on the priests' office, he was guilty of self-presumption. His disobedience over the slaughter of the Amalekites resulted in his rejection by Samuel, who "*came no more to see Saul,*" and by God, who "*repented that he had made Saul king over Israel*" (1 Samuel 15:35). After the first two years of his prosperous reign, Saul's life was one long tragedy in which he went from bad to worse.

"Oh," exclaims Thomas Shepard, "the grievous shipwrecks of some great ships! We see some boards and planks lying in the mud at low water, but that is all!" Just so does Saul's subsequent, disappointing history read. In fits of violence and frenzy, he massacred the priests and hunted his own son-in-law, David, to slaughter; although in his better moments, Saul manifested a strong affection for him. Ultimately, he received the stern rebuke of heaven, the death warrant of the royalty of his own house: "*Thou hast rejected the word of the Lord, and the Lord hath rejected thee from being king*" (1 Samuel 15:26). What an ignoble end to a noble beginning! For us the warning is clear, "*Let him that thinketh he standeth take heed lest he fall*" (1 Corinthians 10:12).

---

21. Thomas Hunter Weir, "Saul," in James Orr, ed., *The International Standard Bible Encyclopedia*, vol. 4 (Chicago: The Harvard-Severance Company, 1915), 2700.

AT THE WITCH'S CAVE

Rejected by God, possessed of an evil spirit, at war with the Philistines, and with no Samuel in the flesh to guide him, Saul felt the chill shadow of disaster facing him and dared not go into battle without some kind of light from the other world. With the loss of the usual means of consulting the divine will, he turned to a necromancer. What a lamentable decay of character! From God to a witch—from heaven to hell—but it is always thus with those who leave God out of their plans. Saul's courage had gone, and he could not pray, for he felt that God had departed from him. And so, in his extremity, he turned to forbidden quarters—to an evil source he himself had previously tried to expel from the land. He had forbidden all witchcraft, but now, in his desperation and melancholy, in the hour of gloom and agony, he turned for guidance to the very practice he had sought to stamp out.

The wretched witch, or medium, and the more wretched king stood face-to-face. But the occult advice brought no relief to his distraught heart, for Samuel's voice only reiterated Saul's fears and pronounced his doom. He received no gleam of hope, only his death knell. "*To morrow shalt thou and thy sons be with me*" (1 Samuel 28:19). In silence, the dejected monarch wrapped his robe around himself and passed out into the dark night. His name, Saul, means "the one who asked insistently, or importunately," or "the beggar." If only he had always sought God, had always prayed always as a beggar dependent upon Him for all things, how different his end would have been.

ON MOUNT GILBOA

From the witch at Endor, Saul, a godforsaken man, went forth to meet his doom at Mount Gilboa. (See 1 Samuel 31.) On the heights, he met the Philistines, and in the midst of a shower of arrows, the end came. Standing at bay before his foes, he had to witness the deaths of his three sons, including his beloved Jonathan. By his side lay his own armorbearer, dead. Weak from the loss of blood, he leaned upon his spear and died by his own hand. Saul ended his sovereignty by committing suicide. The next morning, his armor was fastened above the pagan altar of Ashtaroth. His head, which had always been visible above those of his fellows, was severed from his shoulders and deposited in the house of Dagon. His body was strung up on the walls of Bethshan like a captured bird.

With the fall of Saul, Israel lost a hero whose career had begun with brilliant promise. He had been called to do great things, was naturally talented, and was richly gifted, bold, and valiant. At the outset, he displayed a reverence for God. But he thought of God less and less and became self-reliant until, godforsaken, he was befallen by retribution and died disgraced. Under cover of night, some of his valiant men took down his body and the bodies of his sons and buried their bones under a tree at Jabesh. What a terrible end for a king!

When David received the news of Saul and Jonathan's tragic deaths, he lamented over their passing and uttered one of the most beautiful and eloquent eulogies in literature: *"Saul and Jonathan were lovely and pleasant in their lives, and in their death they were not divided: they were swifter than eagles, they were stronger than lions"* (2 Samuel 1:23; see also verses 17–27).

Let us reflect on Saul's sad story, for there are lessons for our own safety we can glean from it.

1. WE ARE REMINDED OF THE PROBATIONARY CHARACTER OF LIFE

Saul was on trial and, as king, had tasks to perform and responsibilities to meet and discharge that required certain gifts and endowments. But when God calls, He equips; and thus He provided Saul with all he needed. If ever God was patient with a man, it was with this son of Kish, who had such an auspicious beginning. With a wise counselor like Samuel to warn him of dangers, and with the inward ministry of the Spirit, he had a fair chance of success. Just so, all of us have a fighting chance of making good. Is it not a mark of true greatness if we can rise above our evil environment? Triumph shapes character, but to yield to forces that are alien to God's will means loss of soul and exile from God. The span of life is our probationary period, with life as a gift from heaven. The question is, are we using the talent, or are we losing it?

Not many lives, but only one have we,
One, only one;
How sacred should that one life ever be,
That narrow span![22]

2. OBEDIENCE IS NECESSARY AND IMPORTANT

Obedience is the touchstone of spiritual success. But Saul was determined to go his own way; and he took it, to his own ruin. The turning point in his career came when he disobeyed God in the campaign against the Amalekites; then he lied to Samuel. Such a manifestation of self-will had a destructive ending. "*To obey is better than sacrifice*" (1 Samuel 15:22), and to obey the will and Word of God at all times earns God's approbation. The Master could say, "*I do always those things that please*

22. Horatius Bonar, "Our One Life."

[My Father]" (John 8:29). He was obedient unto death, even death on the cross. (See Philippians 2:8.)

3. COGNIZANCE CAN BE TAKEN OF THE REMORSE REJECTION BRINGS

The act of grieving friends by repeated slights, affronts, and inattentions usually ends in separation from them. Saul grieved his outstanding friend Samuel, and his departure from the prophet was followed by the departure of his inner Friend, the Holy Spirit. Saul grieved, insulted, and quenched the Spirit. An evil spirit then took possession of him, and his character quickly deteriorated. Habitual disobedience to the voice of the Spirit, refusing His invitations and admonitions, and persisting in what He hates, are suicidal. Coldness of heart, self-accusation, a gradual departure from God, misery, hopelessness, and godforsakenness ensue.

4. THERE IS A BITTER END TO IT ALL

The majority of men have a craving for religion of some sort. If it is not for the God of heaven, then it is for the witch of Endor. The soul's thirst must be quenched, if not by the River of Life, then by the muddy pools of the world. If we have made a mistake, fallen from heights, sinned against heaven, and feel there is no hope, let us not seek refuge in some God-condemned hiding place. Let us not crave secret things—the mysterious, the speculative, and the impossible; but let us obey the clear command of God to repent and be saved from our sins.

An ever-increasing number of people like Saul are deluded into spiritism, or spiritualism, which is a false refuge and is strictly condemned by God in His Word. While there may be an element of trickery in some séances, they can be diabolically real and therefore should be shunned. Roaming evil spirits are able to impersonate the dead, and this is where delusion comes in. Spiritism is a tragic snare, a corrupting influence that draws the soul away from God. Man's only hope is to get back to God, to His Word.

True forgiveness awaits all repentant hearts. In David's poignant lament over Saul's death, there is no word of revenge or bitterness because of the way he tried to kill him. God waits to treat those who despise Him in the same way, namely, with overtures of grace and mercy. Many years ago, an American artist attracted wide attention by a picture he called *The Return*. It depicts a wanderer in rags and tatters coming to a forsaken home in hopeless anguish. Kneeling by the side of a high bed whereon his father lay dead, the prodigal cries, "Too late! Too late!" For him there is no word of welcome and forgiveness. But our blessed heavenly Father waits to forgive and to restore nobility of character ruined by sin. His arms are ever outstretched to welcome those who turn from their disobedience and despair and come to Him in penitence and faith. He is a God rich in mercy.

Though we have sinned, He has mercy and pardon,
Pardon for you and for me.[23]

---

23. Will L. Thompson, "Softly and Tenderly Jesus Is Calling," 1880.

CHAPTER SIX

DAVID AND JONATHAN: THE TWO MEN WHO LOVED EACH OTHER

There are many different ways of approaching the Bible, the crown of literature. Variety is not only the spice of life but also the key to understanding the comprehensive nature of God's infallible Word. One of the most fascinating features of Scripture truth is its record of charming love stories, whether romantic or platonic. We never tire of reading about Jacob and Rachel, Ruth and Naomi, Hosea and his wife, and the matchless love story of God, who loves a world of sinners lost and ruined by the fall. In this present biographical sketch, we consider the superb friendship of David and Jonathan, which is most unusual because it tells of a love that bound two men together in an indissoluble bond.

From the first assertion of their mutual love until the last expression of David's love for Jonathan when he reverently buried his bones, there was never a cloud between them. (See 1 Samuel 18:1; 2 Samuel 21:13.) Their counterpart relationship in the New Testament is that of Jesus and John, the disciple Jesus loved and who became known as "the apostle of love."

We consider David and Jonathan together, seeing they are seldom separated in the Old Testament; and from the wonderful love tie that existed between them, several spiritual parallels can be traced.

THE WEALTH OF LOVE

Among the many aspects of the noble life of David that the sacred record presents, perhaps the most outstanding is that of love. His name means "beloved" and comes from a root signifying "to love." His name, then, was a true expression of his character and disposition, for he possessed a warm, loving nature. He was the essence of love, and so he found himself loved. He drew out the affection of all hearts who came to know him. Is this not so with God? Love is not only one of His transcendent attributes but an integral part of His being or nature—God *is* love! (See 1 John 4:8, 16.)

DAVID WAS LOVED BY GOD

If Saul was man's choice as king, David was God's choice. "*The LORD hath sought him a man after his own heart*" (1 Samuel 13:14). God chose him because he was a mirror of His own warm, pure heart. David had a passion for God, for worship, and for obedience. God said of him, "[He] *shall fulfil all my will*" (Acts 13:22). Such a love was mutual—God loved David, and David loved God: "*I love the LORD*" (Psalm 116:1; see Psalm 31:23). If this was true of David, it was truer of Jesus, who was of the house and lineage of David. He was a Man after God's own heart, as David could not be. He was the beloved Son, in whom God was ever well-pleased. Could He not say, "*He that hath seen me hath seen the Father*" (John 14:9)? He came as the embodiment and personification of divine love. The same mutual love exists between God and His redeemed children.

DAVID WAS LOVED BY SAUL

When we think of these two contrasting characters, we usually call to mind Saul's jealousy and his effort to kill David. But let it not be forgotten that the Bible says, "Saul loved David greatly." (See 1 Samuel 16:21.) This love, however, was not very deep, or of an abiding nature. It was effervescent and easily turned into anger. With Saul, love turned to loathing as he witnessed David's prowess and popularity, and thus he sought to slay the young champion of Israel.

Do we not have a picture here of Satan's attitude toward Christ? If Saul loved David at one time, it is evident that the devil, before he became a devil, loved and worshipped the eternal Son. But as it was with Saul, so it is with Satan; admiration turned to anger, and ever since his expulsion from heaven, he has been bent upon the destruction of Christ, of the cross, and of the true church. Saul's change of heart can also suggest the sad plight of those who have lost the love they had for the Savior. Does not Paul mention those who once loved the Lord but are now enemies of His cross? (See Philippians 3:18.)

DAVID WAS LOVED BY JONATHAN

Longfellow wrote,

All through there are wayside inns,
Where man may refresh his soul with love;
Even the lowest may quench his thirst
At rivulets fed by springs from above.[24]

---

24. Henry Wadsworth Longfellow, *Christus: A Mystery.*

The unique and remarkable love covenant between David and Jonathan is one of these wayside inns where our hearts can be refreshed. No writer is able to surpass Samuel's superb description of the love binding these two hearts together. *"The soul of Jonathan was knit with the soul of David, and Jonathan loved him as his own soul"* (1 Samuel 18:1). They exhibited the exhortation of the apostle of love: *"Beloved, let us love one another: for love is of God"* (1 John 4:7).

There are two references to the quality of Jonathan's love for David:

1. IT WAS DEEP

Three times over we have the phrase *"loved him as his own soul"* (1 Samuel 18:1; see also 1 Samuel 20:17). Truly Jonathan loved his neighbor as himself. There was nothing formal or perfunctory about this love pact. Jonathan took David and all his interests into his heart. He lived for and loved David as no other. Does not such a love represent the love of the individual believer for the Lord Jesus? Do His interests appeal as powerfully to us as if they were our own? It is to be feared that too often our love is selfish and shallow. If we loved the Lord as we love ourselves, we would find our miserable self-life growing less and less.

2. IT WAS SURPASSING

Hearing of the tragic death of Jonathan, David uttered these beautiful words: *"Thy love to me was wonderful, passing the love of women"* (2 Samuel 1:26). David knew a good deal about the love of women. No doubt he was inspired by the love of his grandmother Ruth for her mother-in-law, Naomi. He also knew that womanly love can be fickle, that a mother can forget the child she bore. Jonathan's love, however, was neither fickle nor forgetful. Because of its rich quality, it surpassed female love, even though that is often the highest form of human love.

No matter how others may love us, they can never match God's love revealed in His Son for you and me. "There is no love like the love of Jesus."[25] On the other hand, is our love for Him deeper, purer, and stronger than the affection we shower upon others? There may be a reference to supernatural love in David's praise of his friend's love, that such surging love as he constantly manifested was divinely inspired. The believer's love for God is more than natural love. The natural heart is at enmity with God and alien to His interests. God loved us before we loved Him. Like the Ephesians, our first love for Him wanes—"Firstborn light in gloom decline."[26] But His love, like Himself, is ever the same.

DAVID WAS LOVED BY MICHAL

Although the marriage between David and Michal had been arranged by Saul, twice over we read, *"Michal Saul's daughter loved David"* (1 Samuel 18:20; see also verse 28). We are never told that he loved her. Michal was allocated to David because of his famous slaughter of the giant of the Philistines, Goliath. Being that David was a handsome young man, doubtless Michal found him attractive and fell for him. An aspect of her love that we must not overlook is that she professed it in a home antagonistic to David. Further, it was her love that foiled Saul's angry attempt on the life of her husband. True love is always ingenious in the defense of its own. Becoming the bride of the one she loved, Michal can represent the love of the true church for her heavenly Bridegroom. We live in a world hostile to Jesus, in which men still try to destroy Him; and our obligation is to

25. W. E. Littlewood, "There Is No Love like the Love of Jesus," 1857.
26. George W. Robinson, "I Am His, and He Is Mine," 1876.

declare our love to Him and prove it in utter devotion to His cause.

DAVID WAS LOVED BY ALL ISRAEL AND JUDAH

The courageous and commendable ways of David created universal attraction. Everyone was drawn to him by love, as filings to a magnet. After Samuel pronounced David heir to the throne, jealousy ensued, and two factions arose—those who followed Saul and those who followed David. But the day came when all the tribes were united, and anointed him king over all the tribes; and for thirty-three years he reigned over both Israel and Judah. In this reign over all Israel, we have a foregleam of the day when all God's ancient people will unite to recognize, love, and serve Jesus as their King. He came as their King almost two millennia ago, but they would not have Him reign over them, and they crucified Him. Over His cross was written, "*This is Jesus the King of the Jews*" (Matthew 27:37). Yet the day is coming when all the scattered tribes will be regathered, and they will fall at His feet and, seeing Him whom they pierced, will adore and magnify Him.

Thus our blessed Lord, because of His eternal love, draws all to Himself. Jonathan never tired of telling David how he loved him. A thousand times a day may we be found saying from our heart, "I love the Lord." Out of our adoration for His sacrificial love, may He continually hear the sincere confession, "My Jesus, I love Thee, I know Thou art mine."[27]

When He puts to use the old-time question "*Lovest thou me...?*" may ours be the instant reply, "*Thou knowest that I love*

27. William R. Featherston, "My Jesus, I Love Thee," 1864.

thee" (John 21:15, 17). If He has the love of a heart true and clean, then He will have possession of the lover himself.

THE SPRING OF LOVE

Having considered the wealth of love showered upon David by all who had contact with him, we now come to examine the reasons why such love was manifested toward him. As we have seen, Jonathan is pictured as loving David with a deeper, holier love than any other could give. What was the cause of such untainted, unselfish affection? Well, we must take into account what happened after David's victory over Goliath. "*And Saul took* [David] *that day, and would let him go no more home to his father's house*" (1 Samuel 18:2). This meant that the two lads were thrown into daily contact with each other, and what a contrast there was between the two—the young, strong, brave, good-looking yet poor shepherd lad on the one hand; and the rich young prince of Israel on the other. David was taken out of poor, lowly circumstances and made a member of the royal household—a picture of the condescending love and grace of God in taking poor, insignificant creatures and making them members of His royal household. Having entered His banqueting house of love, we go no more to the old haunts.

The deep, loyal love of Jonathan for David was not causeless. How did it spring up? How was it first begotten or cultivated? Why did he love him as his own soul? Such an effect must have had a cause, although with God's love for us, it is different. The only reason we can give for setting His love upon us is "*because the* Lord *loved* [us]" (Deuteronomy 7:8). As they were so unlike Him, there was nothing in His people of old to draw out His love to them. But parallels can be traced in the ways David was loved by those around him.

HE WAS LOVED BECAUSE OF HIS LOVE

This reciprocal love is evident in the phrase "*The soul of Jonathan was knit with the soul of David*" (1 Samuel 18:1). Like answered to like. Each gave what he got. As both had the same divine quality of love, there came the union of two kindred hearts. The phrase "*was knit*" implies "bound up." This strong term is also used of Jacob's love for his motherless son, Benjamin: "*Seeing that his life is bound up in the lad's life*" (Genesis 44:30). Aristotle remarked that two true friends are called one soul. The old Anglo-Saxon word for *knit* is akin to our English word *knot*. *Knitting* a garment means "interlacing," or "bringing and binding together single yarns, thereby making them one." It was a love knot that made David and Jonathan one.

David's deep, affectionate, warm, and generous heart responded in full measure to the abandonment of Jonathan's love. Each had the same divine quality, which resulted in the union of kindred hearts. The two youths were knit together in their desires and interests as the warp and woof of web. Their vital aspirations were intertwined, producing a wonderful unity of hope and purpose.

The marvelous love of David is seen in his forced parting from Jonathan. "*They kissed one another, and wept one with another, until David exceeded*" (1 Samuel 20:41). Those abundant tears proved the abundance of love. Perhaps because David was the younger of the two, his love was fresher. Does not all this suggest our relationship to Christ? As David's tears exceeded Jonathan's, so the Redeemer's tears over us exceed the tears we shed over our sinful selves. "*We love him, because he first loved us*"

(1 John 4:19). Through grace, the Lord and I are knit together and made one. By the Holy Spirit, there has been formed a mystical union between us, and we are eternally one.

HE WAS LOVED BECAUSE OF HIS LOVELINESS

David was not only loving but lovely. Many of us are the latter but not the former. Yet, after all, beauty of character is more commendable and enduring than beauty of face and form. But David was fortunate in that "*he was ruddy, and withal of a beautiful countenance, and goodly to look to*" (1 Samuel 16:12). Who could resist loving such a well-built, handsome, fresh-colored youth? At the time when the two first met, Jonathan would have been about forty and David around sixteen or seventeen years of age. David, therefore, had the bloom of beauty, the freshness and fairness of youth, and this called out Jonathan's love. David was a child of nature, living in the fields, mountains, and valleys; and this was reflected in his beauty and in the glow of his countenance.

Do we not love the Lord Jesus with a deep and ever-deepening love because of His loveliness? He retained the beauty of His youth, for He was but thirty-three years of age when His lovely visage was marred more than any man's. Renowned though David was for his handsomeness, he could say of the Lord, "[He is] *fairer than the children of men*" (Psalm 45:2). Solomon said, "*My beloved is white and ruddy, the chiefest among ten thousand....He is altogether lovely*" (Song of Solomon 5:10, 16). Zechariah exclaimed, "*How great is his beauty!*" (Zechariah 9:17). Such beauty is eternal, for no wrinkles gather on His brow; old age does not disfigure Him. He will ever be the "fairest of all the earth beside."[28] The tragedy is that the vast majority see "*no beauty that* [they] *should desire him*" (Isaiah 53:2). To

28. Manie P. Ferguson, "That Man of Calvary," 1904.

their sin-blinded eyes, *"he hath no form nor comeliness"* (Isaiah 53:2). As the Creator of all that is lovely and beautiful in the world, what must He Himself be like? Because of all He is in Himself, He captivates our hearts; and with Peter, we confess, *"Thou knowest that* [we] *love thee"* (John 21:15, 17).

HE WAS LOVED BECAUSE OF HIS LIFE

"Beauty," we say, "is only skin deep." This is why a beautiful life is more impressive than a beautiful face. Jonathan's heart was captured by the character of this man after God's own heart, for David knew how to "behave himself wisely." (See 1 Samuel 18:14.) It is written of him that he was *"prudent in matters, and a comely person, and the LORD* [was] *with him"* (1 Samuel 16:18; see also 1 Samuel 18:14–15, 30). To friend and foe alike, he manifested nobility of character. Except in the matter of Uriah, he was above reproach, discreet, wise, and kind in all matters. Such a life was not the product of self-culture but of communion, for he lived with the God of nature and of revelation. Love for the Lord elevated his stature and made him gentlemanly.

The very mention of David's name stirred Jonathan's breast. Is this not so with David's greater Son, who was ever prudent, comely, circumspect, and upright? Do we not love Christ because He is holy, harmless, and undefiled? He was without fault during His earthly sojourn, as even His enemies confessed. (See, for example, John 19:6.) He is God's spotless Lamb, earth's first perfect Gentleman. David's remarkable life made his own name precious: *"His name was much set by"* (1 Samuel 18:30). It was an ointment poured forth and uttered with reverence and loved by all. Likewise, our blessed Lord has *"a name which is above every name"* (Philippians 2:9; see also Isaiah 52:13), a name so sweet in a believer's ear. As David's personal attractiveness and fragrant life drew out Jonathan's affection, so may we be found lavishing our love upon a greater Man than David, who lived and spoke as no other man.

> Let me love Thee, love is mighty,
> Swaying realms of deed and thought;
> By it I shall walk uprightly,
> I shall serve Thee as I ought.[29]

HE WAS LOVED BECAUSE OF HIS LABORS

The record says that David was "*cunning in playing, and a mighty valiant man, and a man of war*" (1 Samuel 16:18). He was both musical and mighty. A poet and a player of no mean order, he became known as "*the sweet psalmist of Israel*" (2 Samuel 23:1). That melody and harmony were in his heart can be seen in the matchless psalms he composed. In his mad fits, Saul knew how soothing David's playing on the harp could be. That he was valiant as well as vocal, mighty as well as musical, is evidenced by his triumphs over foes, especially his victory over Goliath. Jonathan's love, then, was fed by the rich musical gifts and marvelous exploits of David. The noble prince could not help loving such a man.

Again we have a comparison between David and our Lord. At the outset of creation, did not the Lord instruct man how to invent musical instruments and play them? (See Genesis 4:21–22.) Is He not the one who puts a new song in our mouth? (See Psalm 40:3.) As David's harp calmed Saul in his melancholy moments, so "the Name of Jesus sounds [sweet] in a believer's ear. It soothes his sorrows."[30] Into songless lives in a sad world, He comes with the song of salvation; and as the sinner, whose sin causes the harp to hang on a willow tree, repents, His is the gentle voice heard urging the pardoned one to take down the

29. Herbert Howard Booth, "Let Me Love Thee, Thou Art Claiming," 1899.
30. John Newton, "How Sweet the Name of Jesus Sounds," 1779.

harp and sing a new song unto Him. Then who is as valiant and mighty as He? A man of war, He fought a grimmer contest than that of David with Goliath. At Calvary, He destroyed the works of the devil. When He cried, *"It is finished"* (John 19:30), He meant that He had laid hold of the principalities and powers of hell and robbed them of their power and authority. By dying, He secured a blood-bought victory for us and consequently merits our heart's full love.

What else could Saul, Jonathan, and all Israel do but love David after his great and glorious victory over the giant, which raised him above Saul in courage and in faith in God? The maidens sang that while Saul slew his thousands, David had ten thousands to his credit. (See 1 Samuel 18:7; 29:5.) It was this noble deed that bound Jonathan to David until Saul and his sons were finally slain by the Philistines. David met Goliath *alone,* and Jesus met the forces of hell at the cross in the same way. He fought the giant of the caverns of darkness alone and now enables us to follow Him in the train of His triumph. *"The men of Israel and of Judah arose, and shouted"* (1 Samuel 17:52) when Goliath fell. It is easier to shout than to fight. David killed the giant with his own sword. The devil had the power of death, and Jesus defeated him with his own sword. "Death, by dying, slew,"[31] and we praise Him for His all-glorious deed. David was versatile, having a variety of gifts. He was expert as a shepherd, singer, and sovereign. Job could say to the Lord, *"I know that thou canst do every thing"* (Job 42:2). And increasingly, we love Him because He is able to deal with the giants of doubt, despair, and defeat that we meet on our pilgrimage.

31. Samuel W. Gandy, "His Be the Victor's Name," 1838.

HE WAS LOVED BECAUSE OF HIS LOWLINESS

Another cause of the warm, deep, and abiding love of Jonathan for his young friend was his humility. Lowly, unassuming, and unassertive, David was doubly attractive. Despite the honor heaped on him, he remained humble. He never spoke of or bragged about his defeat of Goliath. Others praised him for his bravery, but you will search the sacred record in vain for any explicit reference from his own lips to the valiant exploit that saved Israel from her foes. (See 1 Samuel 18:7; 21:9; 29:5.) *"Let another man praise thee, and not thine own mouth; a stranger, and not thine own lips"* (Proverbs 27:2). How David's humility shines in his single-handed combat with the defiant, godless Goliath! David knew that he was only the instrument God used to achieve such a victory, so he gave all the glory to Him, saying, *"The battle is the LORD's"* (1 Samuel 17:47). When he appeared before King Saul for commendation and reward, he did not boast. Not ashamed of his lowly estate, he said, *"I am the son of thy servant Jesse"* (1 Samuel 17:58).

Lifting our thoughts higher, do not we love Jesus for His lowliness? Was He not *"meek and lowly in heart"* (Matthew 11:29)? A study of His earthly sojourn reveals that He was a complete stranger to a proud or boastful spirit. Certainly in His great "I ams" (see John 14:6; 18:6), we have His self-assertion of deity, but His claims were made without any trace of self-assertiveness. After His resurrection, He had little to say about the marvelous deed at Calvary. The fact that He was alive forevermore spoke for itself. The apostles could sing praises to Him as the Victor divine, but they magnified Him for His humility: *"Christ...though he was rich, yet for* [our] *sakes he became poor"* (2 Corinthians 8:9).

The lesson for our own hearts at this point is that if we would attract the love of others, we must follow David and David's Lord. Pride is a sin God hates; and boastfulness, self-glory, and self-assertiveness must have no place in our witness. "*Let another praise thee, and not thine own mouth*" (Proverbs 27:2). To seek our own glory is no glory at all. (See Proverbs 25:27.) Lowliness is not only attractive but blessed, for "*he that humbleth himself shall be exalted*" (Luke 14:11).

Forbid it, Lord, that I should boast,
Save in the death of Christ, my God!
All the vain things that charm me most,
I sacrifice them to His blood.[32]

THE COVENANT OF LOVE

Having considered the bounteous wealth of love bestowed upon David, and his personal qualities responsible for such universal attraction, we now come to examine the wonderful love covenant Jonathan and David entered into. Their mutual love resulted in a sacred vow: "*Then Jonathan and David made a covenant, because he loved him as his own soul*" (1 Samuel 18:3). An interesting fact that emerges from such a covenant is that, suggested by Jonathan and willingly and lovingly entered into by David, the Lord was also a party in it. "*Thou hast brought thy servant into a covenant of the* Lord *with thee*" (1 Samuel 20:8; see verse 16). Scripture records that David consistently fulfilled his part of the covenant, even after Jonathan's death. "*The king spared Mephibosheth, the son of Jonathan…because of the* Lord*'s oath that was between them*" (2 Samuel 21:7).

Such a solemn, mutual covenant suggests two precious thoughts for our redeemed hearts.

---

32. Isaac Watts, "When I Survey the Wondrous Cross," 1707.

1. THERE IS THE LOVE COVENANT OF CALVARY

It was because God loved us that He entered into a holy covenant with His beloved Son in eternity past to redeem us from sin, and the cross was the fulfillment on the Savior's part of such a love bond. Therefore, sinners can be saved in virtue of the finished work of the covenant-keeping Lord. The Lord's Supper is a memorial or covenant feast, and our participation in it is our part of the covenant. *"This do in remembrance of me"* (Luke 22:19). The table declares Jesus as the covenant-keeping Lord and the believer as a covenant-keeping servant. Before long, He will return to gather to Himself all those with whom He has made a covenant. The nature of this covenant is such that it cannot be broken, for it is eternal.

2. THERE IS THE LOVE COVENANT OF SAINTS

As love is the foundation of all divine covenants with man, so love is the basis of all godward human covenants. Every holy vow we take upon ourselves is born as a result of our heart's deep love for Jesus. As the mutual affection of two kindred spirits culminates in the sacred marriage bond, or love knot, so true love for the Lord constrains us to seek an ever closer bond, or union, with Him, and a fuller allegiance to Him. The love covenant between Jonathan and David involved three general obligations, all of which have a parallel in a divine relationship.

THE PROTECTION OF DAVID

It was because of Saul's jealousy and his repeated attempts to slay David, the Lord's anointed one, that Jonathan entered into such a love pact. He told David, *"Saul my father seeketh to kill thee...hide thyself"* (1 Samuel 19:2). And David responded, *"Thou shalt deal kindly with thy servant"* (1 Samuel 20:8). Jonathan acted as a secret spy; and, gauging the turbulent feelings of his angry father, he knew when to warn David. Thus we have the moving episode in the woods where Jonathan's love for David foiled Saul's hatred, for his part of the covenant was to preserve and protect the precious life of David at all costs. If the love knot has been tied between the Lord and ourselves, the same solemn vow or obligation rests upon us. We live in a world that is hostile to the claims of Christ. The devil hates Him and is bent upon the destruction of His cause. But since we are His, our responsibility is to defend His interests at all costs.

What striking contrasts the narrative affords! *"Saul spake to Jonathan his son, and to all his servants, that they should kill David. But Jonathan Saul's son delighted much in David"* (1 Samuel 19:1–2). The one is out to slay, the other to save. Modernists unite to destroy the authority and claims of Christ; as those who have been redeemed by His precious blood, we delight much in our heavenly Lord. In spite of Saul's persistent animosity toward David, we read that Jonathan always *"spake good of David unto Saul his father"* (1 Samuel 19:4). What a lovely example to emulate! When others speak evil of our Lord, deny His deity, impoverish His infinity, and belittle His beauty, we must be found speaking well of Him, pleading His cause, extolling His greatness, lauding His power. There were moments when the pleading of David's merit by his loving friend changed Saul's feelings toward him. May we, as those in covenant relationship with the Savior, always be found singing His praises, pleading His merit, recounting His achievements, and magnifying His grace! Until we "bless in death a bond so dear,"[33] let us defend His interests and proclaim His virtues.

There is a further application we can make of this love covenant. In the noble act of Jonathan defending David there is

33. Philip Doddridge, "O Happy Day, That Fixed My Choice," 1755.

an example we can follow among ourselves as saints. Jonathan might have withdrawn his friendship from David and sided with his father against the young champion. But no, he pleaded for David and endeavored to vindicate him against the false and ungenerous conception of Saul by extolling his merits. There are those who would have us join them in the chorus of criticism, jealousy, wrong, and harsh treatment of others. They would have us side with them against others who may or may not deserve such handling. Included in the love covenant of Calvary was forgiveness, and we should be more desirous of pointing out the kind, loving things that can be praised in those whom others condemn, and forgive and forget the rest.

THE PRESERVATION OF JONATHAN AND HIS SEED

Another side of the love bond is clearly evident. While Jonathan did his best for his friend and shielded him all through, David never had an opportunity to protect Jonathan, seeing that he was a fugitive, an outlaw, because of Saul's animosity. David would have fought bravely at Mount Gilboa to save from death the man who loved him, but he never had the chance. Yet he fully adhered to his part of the covenant in that he preserved Jonathan's seed and offspring: *"David said, Is there yet any that is left of the house of Saul, that I may shew him kindness for Jonathan's sake?"* (2 Samuel 9:1). *"The king spared Mephibosheth...because of the LORD's oath that was between them, between David and Jonathan"* (2 Samuel 21:7). How royally David treated the lame son of the friend to whose memory he was bound by the solemn love bond they had forged!

The spiritual application of all this is evident, is it not? Our Lord will ever honor His part of the covenant He enters into with His people. If He has our best, His best will be ours. If we live for Him, speak well of Him in a hostile world, and defend and protect His cause, He will fulfill His side of the covenant and undertake for us, preserving, providing, and protecting until the journey's end.

We are apt to miss a precious aspect to the martyrdom of Stephen, who certainly was not ashamed to own his Lord. As this valiant defender of the faith was being stoned to death, he looked up to heaven and saw Jesus *standing*. As the risen Lord, He had taken His seat at the right hand of God, but He rose to welcome the entrance of His brave follower into eternal bliss. (See Acts 7:55.) Stephen had stood up for Him, which defense he sealed with his blood, and so Jesus stood to receive the martyred saint.

If we put Him first, we can trust Him to make all that concerns us His concern, and to protect us and ours. If we love Him above others and strive to follow Him fully, He will show kindness to our seed. Often we fret and worry about our health, business, loved ones, and a thousand and one other things, as if He will not keep His part of the covenant. But "they who trust Him wholly find Him wholly true."[34]

As the covenant-keeping Lord, He will not fail to honor us if we honor Him. If our soul is knit with Him, then the entire responsibility of our life is on His shoulders. Has He not pledged Himself to undertake for us?

THE SURRENDER OF KINGSHIP

If only an artist could depict that love episode in the woods as Jonathan faced his most difficult part in the love covenant David and he were making. Saul was king, and, by every right, Jonathan should have been his heir to the throne. But listen to this noble heart that shared none of his father's jealousy: "*Thou*

---

34. Frances R. Havergal, "Like a River Glorious," 1876.

shalt be king…I shall be next unto thee" (1 Samuel 23:17). Chiding his son, Saul said, *"Thou hast chosen the son of Jesse to thine own confusion"* (1 Samuel 20:30)—or to his loss of heirship. Such a taunt, however, did not influence Jonathan, who willingly surrendered any right he had to kingship. In choosing David as his bosom friend, he had forfeited the crown. What charming self-abnegation he revealed in the act! Willing to be second to David, he entered into a covenant to surrender all claims to the throne; he became a *subject* instead of a *sovereign*. He was willing to decrease in order for David to increase. But dear Jonathan never lived to become the king's "love vassal."

If we own the lordship of Christ, then we must surrender all claims to self-government. Part of the love covenant we make with Him is that He shall be king with others next and ourselves last. If He has the throne of my heart, then grace will exceed Jonathan's desire to be next to David or near to him to serve him, for He has promised that I shall reign with Him when I come to share His throne. (See Revelation 3:21.)

THE SURRENDER OF LOVE

Without doubt, Jonathan stands out as one of the loveliest characters in the Old Testament. He was the sincere, faithful, and constant friend of David, whose love for him was beyond compare. Unlike his father, Jonathan's excellence shone untarnished to the very last. He is one of the almost perfect men in the Bible. Not a single shameful trait is recorded of his life. His utter love for David, once he knew that the son of Jesse would succeed his father as king, is seen in the complete surrender of all he had to David—*"Jonathan stripped himself of the robe that was upon him, and gave it to David, and his garments, even to his sword, and to his bow, and to his girdle"* (1 Samuel 18:4). In such a yielding up of all he treasured, he was certainly true to his name, for *Jonathan* means "given of God" or "the Lord is a Giver," and it comes from a word signifying "to give." So the phrase *"gave it to David"* can be translated "Jonathaned to David." What this wonderful son of Saul was by name, he was by nature. He proved that love lives to give and never withholds its best when giving. There are two phases of Jonathan's surrender of his possessions, occasioned by David's great victory over Goliath. We can note in passing that:

1. IT WAS VOLUNTARY

"Jonathan stripped himself." He was not asked to, nor was he stripped by another, but he willingly, freely, and voluntarily transferred all to David, whose brave deed had captured Jonathan's heart and whose love kept nothing back from the conqueror. Sacrifice is more acceptable when it is willing, joyous, and freely made. Love lives to give, and it ceases to operate when there is no sacrifice. Too often we withhold our possessions from the Giver of them, and He has to come and strip us of them. Christ remains the most outstanding example of surrender that the world has ever known. He *"emptied himself"* (Philippians 2:7 RV) and *"gave himself"* (1 Timothy 2:6). When He came to the end, all He could give was His ruby blood, and He voluntarily gave it for our redemption. In His incarnation, He laid aside the outward insignia of royalty and at His crucifixion yielded up His life. When Jesus confronted the rich young ruler, He besought him to sell all he had, if he would prove how real and deep was his desire to be His follower. But he was unwilling to strip himself, and he clung to his possessions and carried with them a sorrowful heart. (See Matthew 19:16–22; Mark 10:17–27.)

2. IT WAS COMPLETE

Jonathan did not keep back part of the price, as Ananias and Sapphira did. (See Acts 5:1–11.) He had no reserves. As Ornan said to David, *"I give it all"* (1 Chronicles 21:23), so Jonathan manifested a similar surrender. True love never seeks its own but gives and keeps on giving until red with the blood of sacrifice. Jonathan gave David all of his outward garments and accoutrements, which is significant; for to receive any part of the dress worn by a sovereign or his eldest son or heir was deemed the highest honor conferred on a subject in the East. (See Esther 6:8.)

HE GAVE HIS ROBE

The robe would be the beautiful and costly outer tunic worn by people of rank and importance. When the prodigal returned, his father put the *"best robe"* (Luke 15:22) upon him. Such an imposing robe suggested royalty and meant that Jonathan was *somebody*; but stripping himself of it and giving it to David implied that he was willing to be *nobody*. He felt that the young warrior was worthier of it. Because of David's defeat of the giant, he merited the distinction. Have we learned how to surrender the robe of so-called dignity to our heavenly David? Have we laid in dust life's glory dead, that Jesus might have all the glory? Think of the robe of glory He stripped Himself of when He became a baby and was wrapped in swaddling clothes! It is easy to sing, "Oh, to be nothing."[35] Our hindrance to spiritual growth is that we want to be *something*. We love our robe too much to surrender it.

HE GAVE HIS GARMENTS

Doubtless these were the military dress and armor items Jonathan wore when in fighting uniform, and they symbolized his power and prowess as a soldier. They represented what he could do. David needed no such outfit. He tried on Saul's armor but discarded it. (See 1 Samuel 17:38–39.) All he needed was the

35. Georgiana M. Taylor, "Oh, to Be Nothing," 1869.

garment of divine strength to cover him. If we love the Lord, all the garments of self-effort, self-righteousness, and self-strength must go. "Filthy rags," God calls them. (See Isaiah 64:6.) We are only acceptable to Him only when clothed in the robe of His salvation and righteousness.

HE GAVE HIS SWORD

The phrase *"even to his sword"* (1 Samuel 18:4) is impressive, for it accentuates this particular surrender. Because the Philistines had denied Israel any smiths, there were only two swords among the people. *"There was neither sword nor spear found…but with Saul and with Jonathan"* (1 Samuel 13:22). What a treasure, then, this must have been for Jonathan to strip himself of! It stood for his fighting power and was valued for self-defense. But even this was yielded to David, and he must have treasured it above the mighty sword of Goliath, which also became his. For us, the sword can represent self-achievements, self-ability, and self-defense. Yet our heavenly David must have our sword, for in loving Him, we must not be found taking our own way, dealing with our own problems, and fighting our own battles. *"The Lord your God, he it is that fighteth for you, as he hath promised you"* (Joshua 23:10). Therefore, we must submit and lay down our arms. George Matheson taught us to sing:

Make me a captive, Lord,
And then I shall be free.
Force me to render up my sword,
And I shall conqueror be.[36]

HE GAVE HIS BOW

The bow was the famous and favorite weapon among the Israelites, being used for both pleasure and war. In his eulogy

36. George Matheson, "Make Me a Captive, Lord," 1890.

of Jonathan, David eloquently praised his friend for his remarkable success with his bow: *"From the blood of the slain, from the fat of the mighty, the bow of Jonathan turned not back"* (2 Samuel 1:22). For us, the bow can stand for our favorite pleasures, for that which we count precious, whether a possession or a person. In the revival that swept through Ephesus, the curious arts and books the people valued were burned. We must not murmur if God asks for our "bow," or that which gives us fleshly pleasure.

Neither passion nor pride
Thy cross can abide.[37]

HE GAVE HIS GIRDLE

This beautifully formed article was the chief ornament of the soldier and was the support around his waist to hold his sword. When worn, it meant that he was prepared for active service. It was also an essential part of the clothing of the priests. *"Gird them with girdles"* (Exodus 29:9). It was a small part of their equipment, keeping the rest of the armor or clothing bound close to the body, and it can symbolize the small things of life on which so much may hang. Some "girdles" are good for nothing. (See Jeremiah 13:10.) But we are well-equipped for service if God's righteousness is the girdle around our loins. (See Isaiah 11:5.)

When Jesus came to die, He had not even a girdle. When prepared for crucifixion, He was stripped of all. But His surrender commenced when He left the ivory palaces for a world of woe. Rich, so very rich, for our sakes He became poor. (See 2 Corinthians 8:9.)

He parted with His robe, with all outward aspects of royalty and majesty, and was found as a babe in infant's clothing.

37. Charles Wesley, "O Jesus, My Hope," 1749.

He parted with His garments. *"They parted* [His] *garments among them"* (Matthew 27:35). He died to all self-defense. They taunted Him, saying, *"He saved others; himself he cannot save"* (Matthew 27:42).

He parted with His sword. He could have smitten His foes who spat upon Him and came against Him with swords, but He did not.

He parted with His bow. Think of all the eternal pleasures He surrendered when He took upon Himself frail flesh to die!

He parted with His girdle. He suffered nothing, not even the smallest things of life, to come between His Father and Himself.

The one thing, however, Jonathan never gave to David was *himself—his* life! The vow *"I shall be next unto thee"* (1 Samuel 23:17) was never fulfilled, for he gave his life in battle at Mount Gilboa. Thus, he never became David's subject, servant, or love-slave. He willingly gave his possessions but never gave his life. In the last issue, God wants not what we have but what we are, first of all. It is possible to surrender our possessions but not our person—our luxuries but not our lives—our substance but not ourselves. Christ, however, gave Himself. Therefore, the first note in the song of surrender should be:

Take my life, and let it be consecrated, Lord, to Thee.[38]

For if He has the full control of our heart and life, then grace will be ours to strip ourselves of all that He desires or demands.

---

38. Frances R. Havergal, "Take My Life and Let It Be," 1874.

CHAPTER SEVEN

Asa: The King Who Became a Revivalist

The kings of Israel and of Judah were a mixed bag. Some were very good; others were good; some were bad; others were in between the good and the bad. The degree of morality among the people at a particular time depended on the character of the king on the throne. Asa, the son of Abijah and the grandson of Rehoboam and of Maachah, the daughter of Absalom, can be placed in the category of the good kings. (See 1 Kings 15.) He was the third king of Judah after the separation of Judah and Israel. The first ten years of his reign were prosperous and peaceful. On the whole, his kingship was commendable and successful, but as the years went by, he became less and less faithful to God and His law. Toward the end of his reign, he contracted a disease in his feet and manifested lack of faith when *"he sought not to the Lord, but to the physicians"* (2 Chronicles 16:12). After serving Judah for forty-one years, he died and was buried with great pomp in a tomb erected by himself in Jerusalem, the city of David. A zealous reformer, he sought to purge Judah of many evils, and it is in this capacity that we wish to think of him.

The national revival under King Asa reads like a romance. It comes as an oasis in the history of the kings, as well as in the actual life and reign of Asa, king of Judah. *"Asa…renewed the altar of the Lord"* (2 Chronicles 15:8). What worldwide interest would be aroused if one of the kings or rulers of our time should become a fervent revivalist! Yet such a scene was witnessed two or three times in Old Testament days. King Hezekiah was another royal revivalist. (See 2 Chronicles 30.)

The fourteenth and fifteenth chapters of 2 Chronicles must be taken together in our evaluation of Asa's work. In chapter 14, we have the outward prosperity of the kingdom and Asa's superficial reformation. But in chapter 15, we come to a detailed account of the nation's inward and religious purification and rectification. And it is from this chapter that we can gather several striking features of the revival led by King Asa that are applicable to the deep spiritual needs of our own day and generation.

POWER OF A SPIRIT-ENDUED MESSENGER

The opening verse of 2 Chronicles 15 tells us that the Spirit of God came upon Azariah. This prophet received a divine unction to proclaim the message that smote the consciences of King Asa and his people. Azariah went out to meet the king, as John the Baptist confronted Herod, with an authoritative word.

> *And he went out to meet Asa, and said unto him, Hear ye me, Asa, and all Judah and Benjamin; the Lord is with you, while ye be with him; and if ye seek him, he will be found of you; but if ye forsake him, he will forsake you.*
> (2 Chronicles 15:2)

The effect of such a Spirit-given word was tremendous. There came immediate restitution. Oh, the power of a Spirit-filled, Spirit-guided preacher! When preachers act under the Spirit's control, something is bound to happen. Do we pray as we ought that the Holy Spirit may come upon all pastors, teachers, and evangelists? All of us need this divine endowment if we would experience the joy of calling sinners to repentance.

We desperately need a heaven-sent prophet, another Azariah, who, filled with the Spirit, would arise to blister the conscience of the nation with a message of sin and repentance. The revival under John Wesley saved England from a bloody revolution. Well might we pray, "Lord, send us another Wesley!"

A SAD CONDITION OF BARRENNESS

The warning of the prophet Azariah contains lamentable notes revealing the decadent condition of the nation.

NO TRUE GOD

For a long season, Israel had been without the true God. (See 2 Chronicles 15:3.) Of course, God was still there, but the people had obscured Him with their idols. And because of intermittent idolatry, God permitted the surrounding nations to vex His people with adversity.

What truer description could we have of our own nation than this? For a long season now, we have been without the true God. Paul's estimation of the multitudes is that they are without God and therefore without hope. (See Ephesians 2:12.) The apostle declares that many religious professors have a form of godliness but are destitute of its power. (See 2 Timothy 3:2–5.) Today the nations are having a foretaste of hell, seeing they have forgotten God.

NO TEACHING PRIEST

Being without a teaching priest also contributed to the plight of the nation. Priests there were in abundance, but none who had a deep spiritual understanding of the true character of God; therefore, they were unable to teach the people. They were satisfied with the mere performance of altar duties. There was no heart concern for the soul of the people. And what is the curse of the church in our day? Is it not a dead orthodoxy? A cold professionalism has paralyzed the church's efforts. She is not as terrible as an army with banners, because too many preachers who handle the law do not know God.

NO LAW

Israel of Asa's time had known the law but had forgotten or disobeyed it. "*For a long season Israel hath been…without law*" (2 Chronicles 15:3). When nations depart from God and drift into a barren religion, it is not long before they begin to trample down the commandments of the Lord. Turning from the principles of the law, men come to do that which is right in their own eyes. Man's views on life and conduct, and not God's, are followed. So we have the sorry spectacle of nations drifting into tragic lawlessness all because of their godlessness. Surely it is time for God to work, seeing that the people have made void His law!

NO PEACE

How God permitted Israel to suffer for her sins is declared by Azariah in no uncertain terms! "*In those times there was no peace to him that went out, nor to him that came in, but great vexations were upon all the inhabitants of the countries*" (2 Chronicles 15:5).

Religious apostasy resulted in social disturbances, political anarchy, and national disasters. Blood flowed freely because of Israel's departure from God.

What of the times in which we find ourselves? With the constant threat of war upon us, is Azariah's word "*There was no peace to him that went out, nor to him that came in*" (2 Chronicles 15:5) not applicable to a war-weary world? Are there not religious causes for the present tensions? We lay all the blame upon economics or men who are drunk with the wine of power. But does not the Good Book affirm that when nations choose false gods, there is war in their gates? (See Judges 5:8.)

SPEEDY RECTIFICATION OF APOSTASY

To all those who are out to bring men and nations to God, the Spirit-inspired message of Azariah has something to say. While what he proclaimed had a definite application to the desperate endeavor of King Asa to rectify national apostasy, the principles underlying the prophet's appeal are timeless.

THE GRACIOUSNESS OF GOD

Azariah prefaced his warning by telling the king and his people that the Lord waited to be gracious. Promises of restoration and blessing can be found in the words "*The Lord is with you, while ye be with him; and if ye seek him, he will be found of you; but if ye forsake him, he will forsake you*" (2 Chronicles 15:2). Thus, though the people had sinned, mercy and pardon awaited them if only they would turn in true penitence to God. And is this not the message we must unceasingly proclaim? God has been ignored and His counsels despised, yet He waits to bless with His favor all those who humbly seek His face.

THE REWARD OF RESTITUTION

Strength of purpose was necessary on the part of King Asa to bring about a much-needed revival. *"Be ye strong therefore, and let not your hands be weak: for your work shall be rewarded"* (2 Chronicles 15:7). And how bountifully the drastic rectification of Asa was rewarded! The thorough expulsion of all that was responsible for the loss of divine favor met with divine approval. If revival is to come in our time, the hands of rulers and church leaders must not be weak in tackling the sins of the nation. Courageous action is necessary if civilization is to be saved from suicide.

THE BAPTISM OF COURAGE

King Asa, we read, was so overwhelmed by the words of the prophet that *"he took courage, and put away the abominable idols...and renewed the altar of the Lord"* (2 Chronicles 15:8). And it certainly took courage on the part of the king to rectify the wrongs of his nation! Asa was never more kingly than when he turned revivalist and led his people back to God. Let us mark the steps in this wonderful national revival.

THE ABOLITION OF ABOMINABLE IDOLS

Everything alien to the will and word of God was exterminated. King Asa did not entertain half-measures. There was no reservation in his reforms. Idolatry deserves drastic treatment. Idols must be torn from their thrones. And so, whatever the cost of revival, Asa was determined to cut through all that had robbed God of His rightful place in the nation. The only defect in Asa's revival, so far as we can see, was his failure to abolish the "high places," which, although originally used for the worship of God, came to be identified with idolatrous practices.

It certainly took courage on Asa's part to displace and depose his mother, Maacah, from being queen, because of her association with idols. (See 2 Chronicles 15:16; 1 Kings 15:13.) This queen mother was removed from the dignity she had enjoyed and the influence she had exerted. It must have cost Asa a great deal to dethrone such a near relative, but it had to be done. The court had to lead the way in the national revival.

Revival in our time and nation awaits the lead of those in places of trust and responsibility. If an idol is anything or anyone that takes God's place in our life, then some unpleasant work of removal must be faced. Revival means the unseating of all that has unseated God in national and personal life. And the narrative clearly shows that there are two kinds of idols to be dealt with, namely, those that must be destroyed and those that must be displaced.

Is there a thing beneath the sun
That strives with thee my heart to share?
Ah! tear it thence, and reign alone,
The Lord of ev'ry motion there;
Then shall my heart from earth be free,
When it hath found repose in Thee.[39]

THE RENEWAL OF THE ALTAR

Asa's abolition of idols was a negative change; the renewal of the altar was positive. (See 2 Chronicles 15:8.) Polluted by unclean idolatrous practices, the altar had to be purified and then sanctified anew. Its sacred purpose was restored. Offerings hitherto sacrificed to idols were abolished, and divinely ordained sacrifices were restored. (See 2 Chronicles 15:11.)

---

39. Gerhard Tersteegen, "Thou Hidden Love of God," 1729.

Coming to ourselves, we realize that the tragic condition of the church, world, and nation is attributable to desecrated altars. Oh, for a land of renewed altars upon which worthy sacrifices are placed! May grace be ours to renew the altar of the heart and of the home!

THE SOLEMN COVENANT

The sacred historian tells us that "*they entered into a covenant to seek the LORD God of their fathers with all their heart and with all their soul; that whosoever would not seek the LORD God of Israel should be put to death, whether small or great, whether man or woman*" (2 Chronicles 15:12–13). This high transaction of Asa and his subjects is parallel with the National Covenant of the Scottish people to be found in Old Greyfriars, Edinburgh, Scotland. In 1638, high and low affixed their names to the scroll, covenanting to be faithful to God in the resistance of all popish practices.

Have we need to enter into a personal covenant to put the Lord first in everything? If we are conscious of any departure from God, let us get alone with Him and write out our covenant of fuller allegiance. It will help us to mortify the deeds of the body to have before us in black-and-white our decision to live only, always, for our King. Once we have given our word, it is only by the grace and power of the Spirit that we do not go back on it. An eminent saint had as his covenant: "May the appropriation of Christ as Savior and Lord be the unvarying, initial act of each new day!" Is this not a covenant we could copy with profit to the soul?

THE REDEDICATION OF OLD VESSELS

What a day it must have been when King Asa "*brought into the house of God the things that his father had dedicated, and that he himself had dedicated, silver, and gold, and vessels"* (2 Chronicles 15:18). Sons who get on in the world are apt to throw off the restraints of a religious upbringing. The godliness of parents belongs to a past generation. Success in worldly matters is not compatible with ways that are too straitlaced. Such is the philosophy of many who have left homes in which God was honored. But Isaac re-dug the wells of his father. And Asa had to bring back into the house of God the things his father had dedicated. All of this is a fruit of revival.

Are these not days when we have need to get back to our first love? Have we not lost our early glow and joy? We have need to return to faith and fervency. *"Thus saith the LORD, Stand ye in the ways, and see, and ask for the old paths, where is the good way, and walk therein, and ye shall find rest for your souls"* (Jeremiah 6:16).

DIVINE BLESSING AND REWARD

True to Azariah's declaration, God was found of them that sought Him. *"If ye seek him, he will be found of you"* (2 Chronicles 15:2). In verse 15, we have two key phrases indicating how the people responded to the prophet's appeal: *"They had sworn with all their heart, and sought him with their whole desire."* Consequently, *"he was found of them."*

The employment of trumpets, cornets, and voices (see 2 Chronicles 15:14) declared the united and joyful determination of the people to abide by their covenant. Thus there came streams of blessing and prosperity from the rectified life of king and nation. Although Asa lapsed in his faith, as chapter 16 shows, he remained free from idolatry to the end of his days. As the result of the revival, *"the heart of Asa was perfect all his days"* (2 Chronicles 15:17); and, therefore, he enjoyed divine favor through the years. Here is the double reward of adjustment to the will of God:

A HARVEST OF SOULS

With idols abolished and the altar renewed, there "*fell to* [Asa] *out of Israel in abundance* [foreigners], *when they saw that the* LORD *his God was with him*" (2 Chronicles 15:9). Both Jews and strangers felt the impact of the revived and quickened life of Asa and his court. And thus is it with ourselves. If multitudes are not in the "*valley of decision*" (Joel 3:14), is it not partly because we have little evidence of being God-possessed and God-inspired?

When God is in the midst of His people, exalted, ungrieved, and unhindered, souls come to Christ in abundance. As the glory of the Lord is revealed, all flesh sees it together. Revival, which represents the quickening of God's people, always results in the ingathering of the lost round about. Blessed ourselves, we are made a blessing to others.

A SEASON OF REST

King Asa experienced material blessings as well as spiritual ones as he swung his nation back to God. "*The* LORD *gave them rest round about*" (2 Chronicles 15:15). "*There was no more war*" (verse 19).

Actual wars will cease only as nations learn how to please God. A world as war-weary and blood-drenched as ours can experience rest and peace only as responsible rulers follow King Asa in his thorough extermination of all that is alien to God's holy will. A Holy Spirit revival is the only force that can calm the restlessness of our age.

Coming to the narrower world of our own life, we can enjoy *"rest round about"* and be free from strife and conflict only as we live in harmony with God's purposes. The question is, are we willing and ready to pay the price of personal revival? Victory and blessing can be ours only as we fully surrender all that hinders. *"Up, sanctify* [yourselves]" (Joshua 7:13) is the divine charge we must obey if the Lord is to do wonders in our midst. Irrespective of who or what led us away from complete abandonment to the divine will, we must take courage and put away our idols, then renew our altar.

CHAPTER EIGHT

HEROD: THE ROMAN RULER WHO MURDERED A GODLY PROPHET

Because of the variety and value of its contents, the Bible is the most remarkable book in the world. It contains some of the darkest and most fearful tragedies ever enacted, the cruelest of all being the murder of the holy, innocent Jesus in cold blood at Calvary. The tragedy we are to consider here is perhaps the most outstanding one other than the grim cross in New Testament history. The chief actors in this terrible drama can symbolize those bound together in a tragedy enacted on the stage of every soul.

Herod was the weak, wicked, licentious king. His name means "son of a hero." "Son of hell" would have been more appropriate.

Herodias was an adulteress, a passionate and lustful woman, and a cruel-hearted she-devil if ever there was one.

Salome was the beautiful yet debased, immoral daughter of Herodias and the willing tool of her wicked, conniving mother.

John the Baptist was the stern, fearless, and faithful witness and messenger, who, being in the road of the godless trio, had to be silenced.

Thus, in this hellish scene, we have a mixture of light and darkness, sensuality and sanctity, the fragrance of heaven and the foulness of hell. Solomon, who spoke from experience, wrote, "*He that ruleth over his spirit* [is better] *than he that taketh a city*" (Proverbs 16:32). But Herod could not reign over his lust and, thus devoid of victory in the moral realm, was insensible to, and incapable of responding to, higher things. This member of the famous—or infamous—Herod family was Herod Antipas, the son of Herod the Great and Malthace, a Samaritan woman. Thus he had a drop of Jewish blood in his veins. Galilee of the Gentiles was a fitting dominion for a prince who was far from princely. Let us try to trace the steps in his wicked career.

UNLAWFUL POSSESSIONS

John the Baptist, troubler of Herod's conscience, told him bluntly that he was living in sin. "*It is not lawful for thee to have thy brother's wife*" (Mark 6:18; see also Leviticus 18:16; 20:21). He was, of course, referring to Herodias, wife of Herod's brother Philip, whom Herod had seduced while in Rome. His marriage to this evil woman was doubly incestuous in that her first marriage was with her uncle, and her second marriage with Herod was entered into while her first husband, from whom she was not divorced, was still living. Furthermore, Herod's lawful wife, whom he had banished to her father's home at Petra, was also still living. Thus it was doubly unlawful for him to take Herodias as a wife. What an immoral tangle!

But the Baptist, who came upon the scene in the spirit and power of Elijah, whose New Testament counterpart he was, courageously condemned Herod's unlawful possession. The Old Testament provides a similar combination of characters: King Ahab resembles Herod; Jezebel, Herodias; and Elijah, John the Baptist. In both cases, we have the king drawn in opposite directions—a strong-willed temptress on the one hand; a stern, ascetic, godly prophet on the other. The application of all this to our heart is clear. Our conscience is our John the Baptist; our corrupt, old nature is our Herodias.

We read in Mark 6:18, *"John...said,"* but the original implies "kept on saying." His stern voice constantly rebuked Herod. A conscience controlled by the Holy Spirit never ceases to remind us of that which is unlawful in our lives. May we not be guilty of living in ways that God's Word condemns! If we are conscious of harboring some dark, hidden thing in our heart or life, let us listen to the divine voice saying, *"It is not lawful for thee to have* [it]," and, by the power God can impart, abandon it, no matter the cost.

CONFLICTING DESIRES

The comparisons and contrasts the Bible provides form a most profitable line of study for those who love the Word. Herod feared John, but Salome pleased Herod. (See Mark 6:20, 22.) There were times when Herod turned his better self to the light. His deep respect for John created a heart that yearned to climb out of the pit of corruption in which he found himself. Observing how just and holy the Baptist was, Herod feared him, heard him gladly, and was exceedingly sorry when he had to kill him. What a stricken conscience Herod must have had when he looked on the blood-spattered head of John!

But although one hour he feared John, the next he was half drunk; and, pleased with the licentious dancing of a scantily clad young woman, with passions aroused, he promised her anything she cared to ask for. Thus, within the king were contradictory voices, and the evil voice prevailed. A John the Baptist and a Herod coexist within each of us. The angel and beast, antagonists as they are, strive for the mastery of the soul. The angel, or the new nature, longs to triumph over the beast, or the old nature. The new nature delights to hear the truth and determines to live victoriously, but then Salome appears, and the lusts of the flesh sometimes win the day. When we would do good, evil is present with us (see Romans 7:21); yet the evil cannot prevail if Christ occupies the throne of the heart.

EASY PERSUASION

The record of Herod reveals how the appeal of lust gains a victory over conscience and God, for in one act he appears to have quenched the light shining in his soul. *"Herod himself...laid hold upon John, and bound him in prison for Herodias' sake"* (Mark 6:17). An inner voice told him to preserve the holy prophet, but he was easily persuaded to yield to the demand of the temptress as she called for the blood of John. How useless it was to admire John yet keep Herodias! He was confronted with purity and passion, and the latter triumphed. Too often, we imprison the noblest and best for the sake of Herodias, or for unlawful desires and worldly company. There are more siren voices saying, "Come and sin" than there are prophets thundering out the warning, "It is not lawful to have the pleasures of sin."

The weak will of Herod was cleft in twain. There were the stern warnings of the prophet in the dungeon, and the foul kisses of a she-devil at his side. It was hard for the king to have the courage of his convictions to pack up Herodias and send her back to her lawful husband. If only he had manifested such a noble trait, what a different portrait his could have been. But no, Herod allowed the clamorous voice of a lustful woman to silence the voice of God through John. We read that the loud voices crying out for the blood of Jesus prevailed over the appeal of Pilate as to His innocence. (See Luke 23:23.)

May we always be firm enough to dismiss Herodias and retain John, and never be guilty of sacrificing John for Herodias's sake! What folly it is to be a slave who yields to sin because of someone else! It may be that Herod thought that the delight he manifested in hearing John would atone, in some measure, for his refusal to part with the woman he had no right to have. There are those who respect the truth and love to hear it preached yet condone sin. Being unwilling to part with the unlawful only aggravates their guilt. Failing to remember that their eternal welfare is at stake, they do not act courageously and independently in the hour of challenge.

SURRENDERED POSSESSIONS

Herod was guilty of believing the folly that he could have the best of both worlds: "He heard John gladly" (see Mark 6:20); "the daughter of Herodias pleased him" (see Mark 6:22). But before long, John had to die, for it is impossible to have both—one destroys the other. If Christ and conscience are refused, then something must fill the void. Does this not remind us of the principle Christ laid down that "*no man can serve two masters*" (Matthew 6:24)?

What a thoughtless, foolish vow Herod made when he was half drunk and roused to passion by the dancing of a low, debased princess in her seductive garment: "*Whatsoever thou shalt ask of me, I will give it thee, unto the half of my kingdom*" (Mark 6:23). Herod is called a tetrarch, meaning that he was a prince or ruler of "a fourth part"; yet he was unable to rule his passions but heedlessly offered to sacrifice one half of the part of a kingdom he governed. Perhaps he thought the temptress would ask for a gold bracelet or costly jewels. But he was forced to shed the blood of the man whose godly conversation he was glad to listen to. Any swine's trough is good enough if a man turns from the rivers of salvation.

The tipsy monarch made a rash promise, a wild oath. He was willing to reward sin with his valued possessions. When men turn their back on Christ, sin makes a full claim, even to "half of the kingdom." They were meant to rule, but their surrender to fascinating sins resulted in their losing their sovereignty and becoming slaves. The Monarch of Love can enable them to be more than conquerors over the Salomes who would captivate their heart and deafen their ears to His voice.

It would seem as if Salome was the only female in a stag party hell-bent on drink and lust, for we read that "*she went forth* [from Herod's birthday orgy], *and said unto her mother, What shall I ask?*" (Mark 6:24). Does this not suggest a reckless disregard of all maiden honor and purity? There are bewitching forces at work around us, and we have to beware, because "*sin, when it is finished, bringeth forth death*" (James 1:15). There is a legend to the effect that sometime after Salome received the head of John on a platter, she fell on the ice, and her head was severed from her body. Whether saints or sinners, we reap what we sow. (See Galatians 6:7). Sin spells retribution. "Chickens," we say, "come home to roost." If men yield to their base instincts and persist in serving sin, the time will come when it claims not half but all of their kingdom, or a soul eternally lost.

USELESS PENITENCE

The heartless murder of John brought the drunken king to his senses, and he was sorrowful over having committed such a foul deed. His tears were unavailing, however, for conscience had lost the power to struggle for the liberation of the angel being crucified in his heart. *"The king was exceeding sorry"* (Mark 6:26). The forces around and within fastened upon him, and he became too weak and powerless to save John's noble head, and that in spite of his tears. But, as in the case of Judas, Herod's sorrow came too late. He had rejected John for the sake of a spiteful woman and for his oath made to her unbecoming daughter, who asked for such a bloody gift.

The question arises, "Should Herod have kept his oath once he heard what was demanded?" Our duty to fulfill an oath depends on the character of the oath we have made. No oath or bond is legitimate if it is unlawful. Shakespeare has the line, "Unheedful vows may heedfully be broken,"[40] and promises that should not have been made should not be kept. Oaths, promises, and bonds against your highest welfare and against God should be repented of, not fulfilled. All contracts with sin and the devil should be immediately broken. If they are not, the conscience will be murdered.

ETERNAL PANGS

Mark goes on to recount that after the slaughter of John the Baptist, Jesus entered His public ministry, and His fame spread, reaching the palace and startling Herod so much as to make him confess, *"It is John, whom I beheaded: he is risen from the dead"* (Mark 6:16). The Greek is emphatic here, implying, "I, I alone beheaded." Herod feels that he alone, and neither Herodias nor

40. William Shakespeare, *Two Gentlemen of Verona* (2.6.11).

her daughter, was responsible for John's cruel death. It was his sin, and he must face its consequences. A sinner can never blame another if his soul is lost. Although it was not a risen John whom Herod heard about, the deeds of those who die in their sin will rise again to condemn them.

What anguish there must have been in the voice of Herod when he mournfully said, *"It is John."* It calls to mind what the lost soul in hell heard: *"Son, remember…"* (Luke 16:25). Yet although Herod heard of the fame of Jesus, His message awakened no response in the king's dead heart. The day came when Herod actually faced Jesus and, acting in a childish way, treated Him as a conjurer; but Jesus kept silent. (See Luke 23:8–9.) Lust, frivolity, and neglect had killed in Herod the desire for a better life. This called forth the silence of Christ. He uttered not a syllable before this incestuous adulterer and murderer of His remarkable forerunner.

The tradition is that Herod was afterward stripped of his power and exiled from palace and kingdom to die in great misery in his banishment. If a man finally rejects Christ, there comes eternal banishment, for *"there shall in no wise enter into it* [the New Jerusalem] *any thing that defileth"* (Revelation 21:27). It is said that when Herodias received the severed head of John, his dead tongue was moving as if speaking in rebuke, and she stilled it. But here that holy tongue seems to speak again to Herod's frozen heart: *"It is John."* By procrastination and neglect, men may stifle conscience and ignore the voice that pleads with them to repent, but the day is coming when it will be too late to respond. Their only hope is to flee to Jesus, even to Him whom Herod saw but refused, and to submerge themselves in His blood, which can cleanse them from all sin.

CHAPTER NINE

Barnabas: The Christian Socialist Who Gave All to Christ

As we are discovering, there is no aspect of Bible meditation as adaptable to our personal lives as that of the biographies of its saints and heroes. How rich and abundant the Scriptures are in their presentation of the character and service of so many of those whose hearts God touched! The Bible is like one vast, grand picture gallery with fascinating portraits painted by the divine Artist. Among those associated with the Christian church in its infancy, no figure is so compelling and charming as Barnabas, a Christian socialist who lived his creed.

THINK OF HIS NAME

Originally Barnabas was called "Joseph"—"*Joses, who by the apostles was surnamed Barnabas*" (Acts 4:36). His new name was a mirror of his nature, for he was a man with a generous heart and a warm spirit. His name has a twofold implication:

SON OF CONSOLATION

The word used here is the same John uses of the Holy Spirit when he speaks of Him as "Paraclete" or "Comforter." Barnabas was an earthly reflection of the heavenly Consoler. What a need there is today for sons and daughters of consolation!

SON OF EXHORTATION

The margin has "Son of Prophecy" or "Son of Counsel." Both of these names fit Barnabas. Such a significance implies that he had received the special gift of persuasive utterance from the Holy Spirit. Later on, we find him exhorting and rousing, encouraging and counseling, the young converts. (See Acts 11:23.) Isaiah mentions that he belonged to the Society of Encouragers. (See Isaiah 41:6.)

THINK OF HIS LINEAGE

Barnabas was a Levite, and, belonging to the separated tribe, he had a slight connection with temple ministry. (See Acts 4:36.) His conversion to the Christian faith proves how rapid and radical its spread was, and how the new evangel broke up the old system of Judaism. Barnabas was one of the priests who became obedient to the faith and left the circumscribed service of the temple for the larger ministry of the gospel.

THINK OF HIS HOME

He belonged to *"the country of Cyprus"* (Acts 4:36), or as the Revised Version puts it, he was *"a man of Cyprus by race."* Cyprus was an island off the coast of Cilicia, and Barnabas was therefore a Hellenistic Jew. Very many from this area were gathered into the church.

THINK OF HIS PERSONALITY

What Barnabas looked like can be gathered from what the native of Lystra said of him: *"They called Barnabas, Jupiter"* (Acts 14:12). This implies that he was a man who had a remarkable physique, seeing as he was associated with a heathen deity who was supposed to have possessed remarkable powers. To those of Lystra, there was no god like Jupiter, before whose overwhelming grandeur and unsufferable awfulness other deities paled. So we can think of Barnabas as a strong, imposing, large man with a correspondingly large heart. Pertinent facts of his entrancing life can be gathered around the following features.

HE WAS A MAN WITH A DEFINITE SPIRITUAL EXPERIENCE

All who would achieve great things for God must begin where Barnabas did—namely, with an unreserved surrender to the claims of Christ. The impartation of a new life principle is always the starting point of the divine Potter as He sets about the shaping of a character. If tradition can be trusted, Barnabas was one of the seventy called and sent out by Christ to evangelize. (See Luke 10:1.) Drawn to the Master by His life, works, and teaching, Barnabas became His avowed disciple.

Converted, Barnabas became fully consecrated, for he sacrificed not only his person but also his possessions. But what, exactly, is behind the statement *"Having land,* [he] *sold it, and brought the money, and laid it at the apostles' feet"* (Acts 4:37)? Under the ancient Mosaic law, a Levite was forbidden to own land; but Barnabas did, and as the result of his deep spiritual experience, he surrendered it. There is, however, a deeper significance connected with that sale of land and the donation of the price received to the apostolic treasury.

In the upper room, while the disciples prayerfully awaited Pentecost, a sacred bond was forged between them, a bond manifested in their being with one accord in one place, and in all of them being filled with the Holy Spirit. (See Acts 2:1–4.) When they later formed into the church, they had all things common—their possessions and goods were sold, and the money was deposited in a common fund for the relief of poorer brethren. This first burst of Christian generosity in the church was the first practice of Christian communism or socialism, in which each was for all, and all for each. *Ellicott's Commentary on the Whole Bible* says,

> The description stands parallel with that of chap. ii. 42–47, as though the historian delighted to dwell on the continuance, as long as it lasted, of that ideal of a common life of equality and fraternity after which philosophers had yearned, in which the rights of property, though not abolished, were, by the spontaneous action of its owners, made subservient to the law of love, and benevolence was free and full, without the "nicely calculated less or more" of a later and less happy time. The very form of expression implies that the community of goods was not compulsory. The goods still belonged to men, but they did not speak of them as their own. They had learned, as from our Lord's teaching…to think of themselves, not as possessors, but as stewards.

Barnabas placed all his sale money at the disposal of the communal fund. Ananias and Sapphira professed to have done the same, but they lied in that they secretly retained part of the price paid for what they had sold. As the result of Pentecost, there was the willing surrender of goods and money. When God gets a man, He gets his money. But the outburst of generosity the apostles experienced came from redeemed men and women filled with the Holy Spirit. Godless, hard, inhuman men, such as what present-day communism produces, can never reach the ideal displayed by the early church in distribution according to need. Barnabas and the rest practiced the purest form of socialism. Among other notable features of this admirable man, the following can be noted.

HE WAS AN APOSTLE (SEE ACTS 14:14.)

This means that Barnabas was a member of the inner circle of those early believers. As an apostle had to be one called by Christ, a witness of His resurrection, and one endowed by the Spirit with special gifts for ministry in the church, Barnabas qualified for inclusion within the apostolate.

HE WAS A GOOD MAN (SEE ACTS 11:24.)

Barnabas must have been a man of deep spirituality to have earned the title Luke gives him. Dean Farrar wrote of "the dignity and sweetness of his character."[41] As *good* is a contraction of God, the apostle was a godlike man. We have differing conceptions of what a "good man" is. If one is just conscientious, having a rigorous morality, we say how good he is. But a lot passes for goodness that is actually self-made and all outward, not inward. Such superficial goodness is mere camouflage. Sometimes it is a deceptive covering for sin. But the goodness of Barnabas was the fruit of the *"good spirit"* (Nehemiah 9:20) and was the evidence of a man made gentle by the gentleness of Christ. Its source was a redeemed heart.

HE WAS FULL OF THE HOLY SPIRIT (SEE ACTS 11:24.)

Nehemiah uses the phrase *"Thou gavest also thy good spirit"* (Nehemiah 9:20). It was from Him also that the goodness of

---

41. Dean Farrar, *Life and Work of St. Paul* (London: Forgotten Books, 2013 [original publication date 1907]), 124.

Barnabas flowed. The word *full* here implies "habitual condition." He was drenched with the Spirit's fullness, God-possessed, swallowed up of the divine.

Is this description true of us? We were born anew by the Spirit, but are we full of Him? Too often, we are fuller of self than the Spirit, and thus we fail to bear His fruit. No fullness—no goodness! It is the Pentecost birthright of every believer to live a life full of the Spirit. Are you claiming the birthright?

HE WAS FULL OF FAITH (SEE ACTS 11:24.)

Faith has been called "a vision and an adventure." As with Barnabas, both can be ours, as well. This son of consolation had no doubt as to God's ability to do everything, or of the efficaciousness of the finished work of the cross, or of the Spirit's power. In his service for the Master, such habitual faith was rewarded.

HE WAS USED TO ADD MANY UNTO THE LORD (SEE ACTS 11:24.)

Barnabas was not a go-getter for members of a church. Rather, he was one greatly used to bring large numbers into saving contact with Christ. The secret of his effective soul-winning was a life full of the Spirit. It is not possible for one fully possessed by the Spirit to be fruitless or barren in service. Additions to the Lord, and even to church membership, are few today. What spiritual dearth we are experiencing! But a mighty spiritual upheaval in pulpit and pew alike would soon alter things.

HE WAS A MAN WHO BELIEVED IN ENCOURAGEMENT

As his name suggests, Barnabas was a son of consolation or exhortation or encouragement. The tendency of modern life is to make us hard and indifferent to the needs of others. Our frustrated society needs more sons and daughters of encouragement. Barnabas excelled in giving people fresh hearts.

HE ENCOURAGED PAUL

After his remarkable conversion on that Damascus road, Saul of Tarsus, who became Paul the apostle, desired to join the company of the disciples. But because of his previous persistent persecution of the saints, many in the church had doubts about the reality of the change in the persecutor's life. Barnabas, however, felt differently about the young convert, for he realized that he had gifts and graces the Lord would use. So although "*the disciples...believed not that* [Saul] *was a disciple....Barnabas took him, and brought him to the apostles*" (Acts 9:26–27). Many young believers lose heart because of the lamentable lack of encouragement they ought to receive from those who are more mature in the faith.

It is affirmed by some writers that Barnabas was a fellow pupil of Saul's in the school of Gamaliel. If this is so, then he knew his old fellow scholar well, and when he heard of his conversion, he took it at face value. How rewarded Barnabas was for his faith in Saul and for his strong recommendation of him to the apostles! One wonders what would have happened to the onetime adversary of the church if Barnabas had not consoled and encouraged him when others rejected him. There comes a moment in the experience of a young convert when he is either blessed or blighted by the actions of elder brethren. We should never doubt the reality of change in one professing Christ but should foster him all we can and encourage him to follow on to know the Lord in a fuller, richer way.

HE ENCOURAGED CONVERTS

As a Hebrew Christian, Barnabas accepted the divine plan to make Jew and Gentile one in Christ. Through believers from Cyprus and Cyrene, a great revival swept through Antioch, and a great number believed and turned to the Lord. The church council in Jerusalem heard of this unofficial religious upsurge and sent Barnabas to inquire about it and to bring back the facts of the case. Being a man of Cyprus, he was the best man to send, seeing as he would likely be known to these revivalists from his native city. (See Acts 11:19–26.) Below is what he found on his arrival at the revival scene.

WHAT HE EXPERIENCED

WHAT HE SAW

The grace of God. (Acts 11:23)

There was no church system or organization in the area. The Spirit of God is not confined to religious bodies and systems. Wherever the grace of God reigns, there the true church can be found. Barnabas saw the grace of God in the mighty ingathering of transformed lives. Salvation is all of grace.

HOW HE FELT

He…was glad. (Acts 11:23)

Nothing can gladden the saints like a marvelous movement of the Spirit among saved and unsaved alike. The cry of the psalmist was, "*Wilt thou not revive us again: that thy people may rejoice in thee?*" (Psalm 85:6). Barnabas had no criticism to offer for what he had witnessed. His heart was filled with unbounded joy. He poured no cold water upon the lively enthusiasm of those young converts. He was a true encourager of the many who had turned unto the Lord.

WHAT HE DID

> *He…exhorted them all, that with purpose of heart they would cleave unto the Lord.* (Acts 11:23)

Is it any wonder that the disciples were called Christians *first* in Antioch? As the result of the gracious ministry of Barnabas, those converts in the city exhibited such Christlikeness that the inhabitants nicknamed them "Christians," or "Christ's ones." For a whole year, Barnabas and Paul taught those new believers and formed them into a vigorous church. (See Acts 11:26.) Does not such a stirring experience of revival blessing make us long for a repetition of God's grace and power in this sin-cursed, sex-ridden world of ours? Well might we pray, "God, send a revival, and let it begin in me!"

HE WAS A MAN ENTRUSTED WITH GREAT SERVICE

Conscious that he had been saved to serve, Barnabas was an apostle who was always active for his Savior. He served, as well as surrendered, to the limit. The great opportunity came when "*the Holy Ghost said, Separate me Barnabas and Saul for the work whereunto I have called them*" (Acts 13:2). Reviewing the witness of Barnabas, we note the following features:

HE WAS GENUINELY UNSELFISH

Unselfishness is always the mark of those who accomplish great things for God. They are not puffed up by their own importance. Although he was older in the faith than Saul (now Paul), Barnabas yet had grace to realize that his companion was meant to occupy a remarkable sphere of service. Knowing that Paul was a far abler teacher than himself, Barnabas sought him out to assist in the spiritual instruction of the converts at Antioch. (See Acts 11:25.)

HE WAS SET APART BY THE HOLY SPIRIT

Called by the Spirit to missionary work, Barnabas went everywhere preaching and teaching the Word. Separation unto service came as the result of his having received the Holy Spirit. There are many in the church today who are trying to serve God and have never experienced His saving grace and power; consequently, they are minus the indwelling Spirit to inspire them for service. Churches may call pastors, but only God the Spirit can *separate* those He desires to use. What folly it is for a man to choose the ministry as a profession, just as another person may decide to be a lawyer! One must be called of God. The Spirit had separated Barnabas, and he started at home. Sailing to Cyprus, he began there and was signally blessed. If we fail to witness for Christ at our own Cyprus, we will not be of much use to Him anywhere else.

HE SUFFERED FOR THE CAUSE OF CHRIST

Along with vast numbers of the early saints, Barnabas found that true service and suffering are combined. It was from Antioch, the city in which he had had so many spiritual triumphs, that, along with Paul, he was expelled, the two apostles being forced to shake the dust off their feet against those who rejected them. But even persecution could not crush their enthusiasm. *"Filled with joy, and with the Holy Ghost"* (Acts 13:52), they went on to Iconium. (See Acts 13:50–52.)

Evangelistic work in Iconium, however, was mixed with trials and tribulations, for Paul was cruelly stoned and left for dead at Lystra. When he revived, he and his companion left the city and traveled on to serve and suffer still more. The church could speak of their *"beloved Barnabas and Paul, men that have hazarded their lives for the name of our Lord Jesus Christ"* (Acts 15:25–26). After Pentecost, Barnabas gave over his land and then became willing to give over, or abandon, his very life. Legend has it that he suffered martyrdom for Christ's sake in his own country of Cyprus.

HE WAS A MAN WHO BROUGHT A SUCCESSFUL LIFE TO A SAD END

How saddened we are to find that our last glimpses of this most captivating man reveal him as being party to a most unfortunate quarrel over a relative! It is true, of course, that all great men make mistakes. Abraham Lincoln is credited with having said, "He who never makes a mistake, never makes anything." But sometimes mistakes can be very disastrous to God's work and to His servants. The Bible never glosses over the faults of saints. It presents only one perfect, flawless life—namely, the One *"separate from sinners"* (Hebrews 7:26). Barnabas became faulty in two ways.

1. HE WAS TOO ACCOMMODATING

It must have been with sadness of heart that Paul wrote of his onetime close associate in missionary labors, *"Barnabas also was carried away* [was too accommodating] *with their dissimulation"* (Galatians 2:13). The narrative is taken up with Paul's censure at Antioch. (See Acts 15:37–39; Galatians 2:1–9.) Peter, although a converted Jew, had no desire to carry out the distinctions enforced by the Jerusalem church between Jewish and Gentile converts to Christianity. When some of the Judaizing brethren approached Peter about this subject, he swung round and would not eat with the Gentiles. Barnabas, although he believed with Paul that there was no difference between Jew and Gentiles in Christ, was also swayed by the Jewish brethren and joined with Peter in his separation from the Gentile believers.

Paul, close companion of Barnabas as he was, condemned him for his lack of straightforwardness and firmness. The son of exhortation had held strong convictions about the abandonment of old laws for the new faith, yet now he turned against those convictions and thereby earned the apostle's condemnation. Too often, principles are surrendered for the sake of obtaining favor. Paul never veered from his Spirit-inspired convictions. He kept every part of the faith.

2. HE WAS PARTIAL

One of the saddest episodes in Acts is the painful final parting of Paul and Barnabas. The latter wanted his own way, and the former thought it to be the wrong one. The sad severance of these two valiant warriors came as they faced their second missionary journey together. Barnabas wanted John Mark, his nephew, to accompany them, but Paul thought he was not suitable for the arduous task. The contention was sharp. A lot of unworthy words were exchanged. "Blood is thicker than water," and Barnabas held to his choice of his sister's son. (See Colossians 4:10.) This young missionary had left Paul and Barnabas during the first missionary tour and had gone to Cyprus, where he was known and where there was less hardship and easier service. Lacking the daring spirit to evangelize strange lands, John Mark left his uncle and Paul, both of whom were willing to throw away their lives for Christ's sake. (See Acts 13:13.)

Paul was firm in his belief that John Mark was not the man for this further sacrificial task. He evidently had the backing of the church. (See Acts 15:40–41.) Barnabas, overly generous, wanted Paul to overlook his nephew's faults and try him again. But Paul was resolute in his refusal, feeling that Mark's absence from the party would assure greater success. Who was wrong? Perhaps there were faults on both sides, Barnabas being too soft and eager to urge the claims of his nephew, and Paul a little too hard on, and resentful of, the young man. Throughout the church age, there has been a repetition of the same regrettable separation of bosom friends over personal as well as doctrinal matters.

The first separation of Barnabas and Paul occured when they were separated together by the Holy Spirit. How tragically different it was when they separated from each other and went their own ways!

When the Canaanite and the Perizzite are in the land, let not Abraham and Lot disagree and part. It is both strange and significant that after his severance from Paul, Barnabas never appears in New Testament history again. The reference in 1 Corinthians 9:6 relates to their united apostleship before the tragic break came. Barnabas retired to Cyprus, where he started to serve the Lord. Through one mistake, he passed out of Scripture and likely ended a life of great usefulness. Such a blessed yet broken fellowship serves as a beacon of light to all who labor for the Master. There are signs that young Mark retrieved his position and afterward became warmly attached to the apostle Paul. "*Take Mark, and bring him with thee: for he is profitable to me for the ministry*" (2 Timothy 4:11; see also Colossians 4:10; Philemon 23–24). Nothing would have pleased Paul more than that he could have written the same about the return of Barnabas as a companion in travel and tribulation. Knowing of Mark's return to Paul, as must have been the case because of the family relationship, Barnabas must have seen how the rigid discipline of his onetime companion had been beneficial to the work.

CHAPTER TEN

TIMOTHY: THE EVANGELIST WHO WAS SUBJECT TO STOMACH TROUBLE

In our glimpse of the portrait of David and Jonathan, we have already seen how two men were drawn together and made as "one soul." A deep mutual affection resulted in an affinity of minds uncommon among males. It is most rare for the one to confess of his bosom friend, *"Thy love to me was wonderful, passing the love of women"* (2 Samuel 1:26). Until Jonathan's death, he and David were all in all to each other. Coming to the New Testament, Paul, the aged missionary and teacher, and Timothy, the young and ardent evangelist, provide us with a further illustration of how two men can be drawn together and "lock'd up in steel."[42] In *Hamlet*, Shakespeare advises, "Those friends thou hast, and their adoption tried, grapple them to thy soul with hoops of steel."[43]

As we are to see, "hoops" of mutual love for Christ and for each other bound Paul and Timothy together in an indissoluble union, with one becoming increasingly dependent upon the other. Such a fellowship of kindred hearts is like to that in heaven. As a good deal of sentiment attaches to the last message

42. William Shakespeare, *Richard III* (5.1.21).
43. Shakespeare, *Hamlet* (1.3.65–66).

of one we greatly revere, 2 Timothy, the last letter Paul wrote before his martyrdom, must have been especially sacred to the heart of his much-loved young companion. How Timothy must have treasured that warm final letter, coming as it did from a warm heart housed in a cold, damp dungeon.

For a full portrait of Timothy, we must string together all that the apostle Paul recorded of the life and labors of his spiritual son, who was many years his junior.

HE WAS THE CHILD OF A GODLY HERITAGE

Timothy was the son of a Christian Jewess named Eunice and the was grandson of Lois. His unnamed father was a Greek and a non-Christian. (See Acts 16:1–3.) It is said of his mother that she *"believed"*; but nothing is said of his father's faith. It may be that both were unbelievers when they married but that Eunice, along with her mother, came to embrace the Christian faith during Paul's first missionary tour to Lystra, where the family lived and where Timothy was born.

It would seem as if the father had died when Timothy was quite young, seeing that his upbringing appears to have been in the hands of his mother and grandmother. The reference to the faith of these two godly women and to the Scriptures in the home indicates the spiritual atmosphere in which the growing boy was lovingly nurtured. (See 2 Timothy 1:5; 3:15.) Lystra was not far from Tarsus, Paul's birthplace, hence his intimacy with the family, his knowledge of the faith of Timothy's kinsfolk, and his unbroken and devoted friendship for the son of the home, his dearest and best-loved partner in the Master's service. In the opening of his second letter to Timothy, Paul urges the young soldier never to forget those home influences responsible for the molding of his youth. Two precious phrases can be linked in this advice: "*my prayers*" (1 Timothy 1:3) and "*thy tears*" (verse 4). Paul was unceasing in his intercession for his son in the faith, and Timothy's "tears" were shed over his friend's departure. This was the last sight Paul had had of him—*weeping.*

The Lycaonians among whom Timothy spent his childhood were heathen worshippers of Jupiter, whose temple stood in the city. It was in this wild region, where Paul first worshipped and later was almost stoned to death, that the seeds of Timothy's education for his great future commenced. Aristotle spoke of the populace as "the inconstant Lycaonians." Yet Paul was to find a convert among them whose constancy he could lean upon. Even in those last days, when he had been forsaken by all those in Timothy's region (see 2 Timothy 4:16), with no man standing by him at his trial, he could send for his young fellow laborer, knowing that, if at all possible, he would hasten to his side and be with him when he was taken out to die.

HE WAS A FAITHFUL STUDENT OF THE WORD

> *From a child thou hast known the holy scriptures, which are able to make thee wise unto salvation through faith which is in Christ Jesus.* (2 Timothy 3:15)

From very early childhood, Timothy had been familiar with the sacred, saving Scriptures. The Revised Version has "*babe*" for "*child.*" The word Paul uses for "*known*" means more than a memory of Scripture, which Timothy was taught to read and receive. It signifies to completely understand or to have an inward perception as to the significance of Scripture. His early training in the Word was received from his mother and grandmother, and Paul urged his Bible-loving friend to continue in the things he had learned and had been assured of. Timothy learned the Scriptures from the lips of the two godly women in the home and was assured of its reality and power by watching its effect in their lives. Thus, lip and life gave the lad a love for Scripture, and his was an undying gratitude for the godly influence of his home. Too few parents these days make the Bible the child's book of letters.

How often, from remotest quarters, from simplest homes, from lowliest parentage, God replenishes the exhausted treasuries of His church! How often a mother's unfeigned faith gives a David Livingstone or a Mary Slessor to the cause of Christ! The responsibilities of those who have known the Scriptures from their earliest days are greater than those who have been bereft of such a privilege. It is an inestimable boon to learn the Word from godly parents. To come to know Christ and His Word later in life and through channels other than those Timothy enjoyed is to start the Christian race somewhat handicapped, especially if the home background was positively unchristian. And yet a person without this upbringing can win the race!

HE WAS PAUL'S CHILD IN THE FAITH

Timothy was only a boy when the two preachers Paul and Barnabas came to town. He was greatly attracted to Paul and deeply impressed by his evangelical preaching, his stoning, and the miracles performed by the courageous evangelist. (See Acts 14:6–7; 2 Timothy 3:10–11.) When Paul returned to Lystra, Timothy had developed into a fine young Christian, being a disciple well reported of by the brethren; and the apostle, observing his spiritual growth and worth, took him on his missionary tour, possibly substituting him for young John Mark, who had proved a disappointment to Paul.

Although Timothy was brought up in a Christian home and was familiar with Scripture from early childhood, he had not made a personal commitment to Christ, and on Paul's visit to the community where he lived, the apostle led him to Christ. Thereafter, Paul referred to him as *"my dearly beloved son"* (2 Timothy 1:2) and *"my own son in the faith"* (1 Timothy 1:2). He said of him, *"As a son with the father, he hath served with me in the gospel"* (Philippians 2:22). It was from Paul that Timothy learned the first rudiments of faith in Christ, and he went on to receive from the gifted apostle his theological equipment as a Christian minister. What a tender relationship developed between Paul and Timothy.

In his most valuable commentary on the book of Acts, Dr. G. Campbell Morgan gives this suggestive description of young Timothy's conversion to Christ:

> At last Paul came to Lystra, the place of stones, the scars of which were still on his body; the memories of the day when they beat fast and furiously upon him were still with him. At Lystra he found Timothy. How often God's servants return, after years of absence, to some rough and rugged place of battle, and of blood, and of agony, only to find the fruitage. When did Timothy become a disciple? The question cannot be answered dogmatically, but the probability is that he became a disciple in those days of Paul's previous visit. Paul had once been a young man, and had watched the stoning of a saint called Stephen, minding the clothes of such as stoned him. He had heard the dying prayer, and the vision of the face of Stephen had fastened like goads in his heart and life. At Lystra he had gone through Stephen's experience; and perchance another man had seen the stones hurled. Now he went back to find Timothy in the place of stones, and from that moment there was formed that

> rare and beautiful friendship, the friendship of an old man for a young man.[44]

The idea has been expressed that when Paul recovered consciousness after being mobbed and stoned, he found shelter in Timothy's home upon his reentry into the town. If this is true, then we can imagine how easily young Timothy would be impressed with the reality of Christ when His servant Paul was willing to be battered and beaten for His sake. Timothy would have been a lad somewhere about fifteen or sixteen years of age when, around A.D. 45, he came to know the Lord. As we have indicated, on Paul's second visit to Lystra, he adopted the earnest young believer as his missionary assistant. He circumcised Timothy out of deference to the Jews so that his usefulness might not be prejudiced by his semi-Greek extraction. Probably he was not circumcised in infancy, owing to the objection of his heathen father. Through Paul's act, it was possible for Timothy to obtain free admission to the synagogue.

HE WAS ORDAINED A MINISTER OF THE GOSPEL

Paul refers to his son in the faith as a *"minister of God"* (1 Thessalonians 3:2) and as *"a good minister of Jesus Christ"* (1 Timothy 4:6). Having been led to Christ by Paul, it was quite natural that Timothy should be ordained as fellow worker with his spiritual father. The laying on of Paul's hands did not impart special gifts to be used in Christ's service; rather, it was the recognition of qualifications already received. Timothy's entrance into the ministry stands out clearly. There was the laying on of the hands of the presbytery and of Paul's own hands. (See 1 Timothy 4:14; 2 Timothy 1:6.) This indicated that Timothy had received the gift of God—the sealing with the Holy Spirit

44. G. Campbell Morgan, *The Acts of the Apostles* (New York: Fleming H. Revell Co., 1924), 377.

as the Spirit of power, of love, and of discipline. (See 2 Timothy 1:6.) Admitted thus to a charge, a trust, Timothy could never surrender it in afterlife without being unfaithful. His call was to a sacred task, lifelong without reservation, arduous, devoted, even perilous; and, true to his name (for *Timothy* means "honor God"), he lived and labored for the honor and glory of his Lord until he finished his course.

Both of the letters Paul sent to Timothy are loaded with practical exhortations as to how the young minister could make full proof of his ministry. Paul desired for him that he might have from God *"grace, mercy, and peace"* (1 Timothy 1:2; 2 Timothy 1:2); and he would need them all in the times of persecution ahead. *Grace* for every service, *mercy* for every failure, and *peace* for every circumstance. "Teachers," said Chrysostom, "stand more in need of mercy than others." Because Timothy was called to an office which carried high spiritual possibility and responsibility, he was, on that very account, more liable to fall short of its ideals, hence the need for mercy.

Ordained thus for the particular work to which he was called, Timothy thereafter enjoyed the intimate companionship of the apostle. He left a loving mother and a pleasant home in which he had every comfort to share in Paul's sacrificial labors. Thus his entrance into a life of service became at once a life of true human fellowship; and from the moment of his ordination, "as a son with his father," he served Paul in the furtherance of the gospel. They became one in their journeyings, in their perils, and in their triumphs for Christ. (See Philippians 2:22.) Such close fellowship of mutual trust and love between these two devoted souls was never severed. In times of separation, Paul yearned for the presence of his child in the faith. *"Do thy diligence to come shortly unto me"* (2 Timothy 4:9). As a traveling companion, Timothy was indispensable to Paul. (See, for example, Acts 17:14–15; 18:5; 19:22; 20:4.) He hastened to gladden the heart of the apostle in seasons of distress, solitude, and conflict. He was the one man nearest of all to the heart of Paul.

HE WAS SUBJECT TO PHYSICAL INFIRMITIES

Paul's advice to his young companion could be practical as well as spiritual. This is evidenced by the fact that Paul urged him to "*use a little wine for thy stomach's sake and thine often infirmities*" (1 Timothy 5:23). What a human touch this was! How solicitous Paul was for Timothy's bodily health as well as for his spiritual welfare. It would seem as if Timothy was not constitutionally strong. J. B. Phillips translates the parenthetical passage to read, "*By the way, I should advise you to drink wine in moderation, instead of water. It will do your stomach good and help you to get over your frequent spells of illness*" (1 Timothy 5:23 PHILLIPS).

That Timothy was in the habit of abstaining wholly from the use of wine is seen in the injunction of Paul not to drink water only but, for medicinal purposes, to mix a little wine with water. Paul favored the general habit of abstaining from strong drink and asked Timothy to depart only to a small degree from total abstinence in order to restore and preserve his health. Too often, this verse is taken to condone the use of wine by those who do not have Timothy's stomach troubles. *Barnes' New Testament Notes* give us a most satisfactory explanation of the apostolic advice:

> [Paul] was giving counsels in regard to an office which required a great amount of labour, care, and anxiety. The labours enjoined were such as to demand all the time; the care and anxiety incident to such a charge would be very likely to prostrate the frame, and to injure the

health. Then he remembered that Timothy was yet but a youth; he recalled his feebleness of constitution and his frequent attacks of illness; he recollected the very abstemious habits which he had prescribed for himself, and, in this connection, he urges him to a careful regard for his health, and prescribes the use of a small quantity of wine, mingled with his water, as a suitable medicine in his case. Thus considered, this direction is as worthy to be given by an inspired teacher as it is to counsel a man to pay a proper regard to his health, and not needlessly to throw away his life.[45]

HE DID THE WORK OF AN EVANGELIST

In his "swan song," as Paul's second letter to Timothy is called, seeing as it was the last epistle to leave his mighty pen, the personal element is strongly marked, and thus contains the veteran preacher's final counsel to a much younger fellow laborer. In no epistle does the true, loving, undaunted, trustful heart of the great apostle speak in more consolatory and yet more moving accents. It is loving but strong and bracing, and having as its object to warn Timothy of heresies multiplying around him in the church and to encourage the young evangelist to prove himself courageous amid all the trials he would encounter as a preacher of the good news of salvation.

That Timothy made full proof of his ministry as an evangelist can be gathered from the way he broke new ground as a pioneer, thereby emulating the example of his spiritual father. (See Acts 17:14.) Enjoying in the highest degree the apostle's confidence and affection, Timothy had the benefit of Paul's constant instruction for his evangelistic labors. (See 2 Timothy

45. Albert Barnes, *Notes on the New Testament: Explanatory and Practical,* vol. 3 (London: Blackie & Son, 1884), 186–187.

2:2; 3:14.) At times, the youthful evangelist was active on distant missions; at other times, he remained behind to instruct and build up converts. Attention is drawn to his service in the crowded seaport of Achaia, where a great spiritual awakening was experienced. (See Romans 16:21.) A glimpse is given of Timothy as an ambassador charged with a delicate and difficult mission to restore a backsliding church—a most responsible task for which gift and grace were required. He also knew how to comfort and establish Christians in the midst of tribulation. (See 1 Thessalonians 3:2.) Timothy's evangelistic ministry thus had a positive and a negative aspect. He was called to win souls for Christ and to establish converts in the faith, thereby building up the church. He was also commissioned to repudiate error wherever he found it by emphasizing revealed truth. Timothy, then, must function as a faithful minister of the Word, a protestor against false teachers, a prophet in perilous times, and a sufferer in Christ's cause.

It may be that Timothy did not have the commanding skill or overwhelming eloquence and literary ability of Paul and therefore was not fitted for a position of first consequence in the church—that is, if we judge from the repeated and urgent exhortation to courage and vigilance that the apostle sent him. He seems to have been of a gentler and even a somewhat irresolute disposition; yet he had qualities of piety and faithful affection, and for a full sixteen years, he possessed the love, deserved the confidence, shared the labors, and alleviated the sorrows of his aged spiritual father. Bishop Handley Moule says this of Timothy:

> His face full of thought and feeling and devotion is rather earnest than strong. But it has the strength of patience, of absolute sincerity, and of rest in Christ. Timothy repays

the affection of Paul with unwavering ability. And he will be true to the end, to his Lord and Redeemer, through whatever tears and agonies of sensibility.

This, then, is the portrait of the young evangelist whom Paul loved, who would be about thirty-seven years of age when his revered yoke-fellow, almost twice his age, laid down his life for the gospel. With the martyrdom of Paul, the curtain falls, and we have no further information about Timothy. We can be sure that he took up the torch and carried it on until death ended his evangelistic labors. Tradition has it that he, too, was martyred, in the reign of Domitian, or Nerva, for his faithfulness as a bishop. While attempting to stop an indecent heathen procession during the Festival of Diana, this God-fearing evangelist sealed his testimony with his blood. He risked and lost his life preserving the "sobriety" he loved to proclaim, and thus he became a "co-sufferer" with his spiritual father in the afflictions of the gospel. (See 2 Timothy 1:8.)

In conclusion, the heart-relationship that existed between Paul and Timothy illustrates the goodness of God in pairing off those who complement each other. David had Jonathan, Elijah had Elisha, with each supplying the other's needs—contrasting characters unified in a bond of mutual affection and allegiance. Thus it was with the veteran apostle and the youthful evangelist we have companied with for a while. Theirs was a unity in spite of diversity of temperament. Paul was impulsive and enthusiastic; Timothy, reflective and reserved. Thus, zeal and constraint were wedded together. Timothy met the intense craving for sympathy so characteristic of Paul's writings. He might have called himself "the disciple whom Paul loved."

The way in which Timothy's life was wonderfully complementary to that of Paul's is touched on by Dr. T. A. Gurney in his study *The First Epistle to Timothy*. There is the deepest unity in its diversity. It is "not like to like, but like in difference." God needed a Timothy to place beside Paul. How weak he appears sometimes against the giant strength of "*such an one as Paul the aged*" (Philemon 1:9). Yet how confessed a source of strength he really was, how necessary and how helpful.

One was a "spiritual father"; the other, a "beloved son." One was born leader of men, a chosen pioneer of a new and untried faith, burning with intensity and zeal for Christ, as once he had breathed out threatenings and slaughter against the servants of the Lord. The other was naturally wishful to be second, not fully sure of himself, and dependent by natural characteristics—a "fellow laborer," not chief.

Paul was so strong, so fully persuaded, and more than a conqueror through his mighty faith. He was sure that, though deserted by men, he was helped by God; and, in authority, he was "*not a whit behind the very chiefest apostles*" (2 Corinthians 11:5). Timothy was so modest in his use of spiritual authority that he shrank back from a self-assertion justified by the duties of his position, till he was in danger of being despised. (See 1 Corinthians 16:10–11; 1 Timothy 4:12.) He needed stiffened up against too easy acquiescence: "Peace-loving man, of humble heart and true!"[46]—the good second, the fervent and constant friend, the man in whom you see, in the mirror, not of the missionary so much as the pastor and overseer of God.

How perfectly these two contrasted characters are interwoven by a common faith and a common devotion to Christ; how much they each owe the other; how complete they are together—these two strings of one lyre that sounds forth the praise of their Savior God. For in undying love to the Crucified

46. John Henry Newman, "Gregory Nazianzen."

One, in self-sacrifice to "make Jesus King" over the whole earth, in the unfailing optimism that knows that the kingdom is sure, because His power and Word are sure, these two hearts and lives are absolutely one.

The Bible saints we have considered knew how to live in "eternity's sunrise," as William Blake expressed it. May ours be a similar endeavor! After cataloging the exploits of the heroes of the past and the martyrs of the then present, the writer to the Hebrews exhorts, "*Whose faith follow*" (Hebrews 13:7). May grace be given to us to plant our feet in the footprints of holy men of old and to follow them in the pathway of love and loyalty to God!

ABOUT THE AUTHOR

When Dr. Herbert Lockyer (1886–1984) was first deciding on a career, he considered becoming an actor. Tall and well-spoken, he seemed a natural for the theater. But the Lord had something better in mind. Instead of the stage, God called Herbert to the pulpit, where, as a pastor, a Bible teacher, and the author of more than fifty books, he touched the hearts and lives of millions of people.

Dr. Lockyer held pastorates in Scotland and England for twenty-five years. As pastor of Leeds Road Baptist Church in Bradford, England, he became a leader in the Keswick Higher Life Movement, which emphasized the significance of living in the fullness of the Holy Spirit. This led to an invitation to speak at the Moody Bible Institute's fiftieth anniversary in 1936. His warm reception at that event led to his ministry in the United States. He received honorary degrees from both the Northwestern Evangelical Seminary and the International Academy of London.

In 1955, he returned to England, where he lived for many years. He then returned to the United States, where he spent the final years of his life in Colorado Springs, Colorado, with his son, the Rev. Herbert Lockyer Jr., a Presbyterian minister who eventually became his editor.